"For there is nothing hidden that will not be disclosed,
and nothing concealed that will not be known or
brought out into the open."

—LUKE 8:17

WHISTLE STOP Café MYSTERIES

APPLE BLOSSOM TIME

RUTH LOGAN HERNE

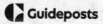

Whistle Stop Café Mysteries is a trademark of Guideposts.

Published by Guideposts
100 Reserve Road, Suite E200
Danbury, CT 06810
Guideposts.org

This is a work of fiction. While the setting of Whistle Stop Café Mysteries as presented in this series is fictional, the location of Dennison, Ohio, actually exists, and some places and characters may be based on actual places and people whose identities have been used with permission or fictionalized to protect their privacy. Apart from the actual people, events, and locales that figure into the fiction narrative, all other names, characters, businesses, and events are the creation of the author's imagination and any resemblance to actual persons or events is coincidental.

Every attempt has been made to credit the sources of copyrighted material used in this book. If any such acknowledgment has been inadvertently omitted or miscredited, receipt of such information would be appreciated.

Scripture references are from the following sources: *The Holy Bible, King James Version* (KJV). *The Holy Bible, New International Version* (NIV). Copyright © 1973, 1978, 1984, 2011 by Biblica, Inc. Used by permission of Zondervan. All rights reserved worldwide. www.zondervan.com

Cover and interior design by Müllerhaus
Cover illustration by Greg Copeland at Illustration Online LLC.
Typeset by Aptara, Inc.

ISBN 978-1-961441-84-2 (hardcover)
ISBN 978-1-961441-86-6 (epub)

Printed and bound in the United States of America
10 9 8 7 6 5 4 3 2 1

APPLE BLOSSOM TIME

CHAPTER ONE

We need to do a complete reset on all three sides of the house if you want to regain control of these plots." Janet Shaw's regretful expression said more to Debbie Albright than her words as Janet studied the tangled gardens flanking Greg Connor's home. The cozy Cape Cod-style building was surrounded by what had been pretty plots at one time. Debbie Albright knew that because the gardens in family photos taken when her fiancé's boys were young looked nothing like this.

The word *jungle* offered a more apt description on this first Tuesday of April. Debbie had asked her best friend and business partner to come by and offer advice. Greg's wife had passed away six years before, and he'd been left to raise two sons, Jaxon and Julian, whose memories of their mother grew fainter with time. By all accounts, their mother had overseen these gardens with the same love she'd shown her family. Debbie was determined to get these borders back into shape.

Janet wasn't known for her green thumb, but the simple and tasteful landscaping around her home indicated she knew something about gardening. That was more than Debbie could say about herself. The combined effect of Janet's tone and expression didn't bode well. Clearly a reset wasn't something to be undertaken lightly.

Debbie mulled over the mess at her feet. The higher angle of the sun had brought shoots to life. A lot of them. Way too many for the size of the plots. She shifted her attention back to Janet. "I have no idea what a total reset means, but it sounds like we're signing up for 'Extreme Transformation, Garden Edition.'"

Janet laughed. "Holly Connor used to call gardening her therapy, and she loved perennials. She appreciated how the house nestles into a mild slope, and she established English country gardens all around the perimeter."

"If this is what gardens look like in the UK, I'm proud to be an American." Debbie made a face. "This isn't a garden. It's a thicket. There must be twenty saplings over there." She pointed to several whiplike things sticking up from the ground. "Even a novice like me knows that can't be good."

Janet sighed. "The gardens were gorgeous through that final year. Even the year after she passed away. She had a knack for making it look unplanned, like the garden just happened along without anyone taking the time to plant it. Not everybody can do that. Then she was gone." Janet grimaced. "The perennials staged a coup, sending out roots and seeds and randomly popping up all over. Then the weeds took over."

"I recognize those." Debbie pointed. The daffodils were in full bloom, nodding bright yellow and ivory heads in the early April breeze. The tulips would follow soon after, that much she knew. Maybe in time for an Easter bouquet. "Everything else is a complete mystery."

"Fortunately, we're good at solving mysteries!"

Debbie smiled and drew a deep breath. "I'm in uncharted water here, and not just about the gardens."

Janet faced her, a puzzled look on her face. "About marrying Greg? And creating a family with him and the boys?"

"Not that, no." Debbie deflected that notion quickly. "Greg makes me ridiculously happy. And I love the boys. They're such good kids. Although they do manage to give their dad a hard time now and again, I have to admit. I bite my tongue, but all in all, they're pretty great. I love them, and that was kind of a surprise too. It's not the people involved." She let out a breath on a whoosh. "It's this. The house. His house. Their house. My house. Changing things. Decisions that can hurt kids' feelings without meaning to. I know it's been over six years since Holly passed away, but of course they still miss her. I don't want to say or do anything that would mess with their healing."

"That's inevitable." Janet always spoke frankly, and today was no different. "I'd love to give you words of wisdom, but hurt feelings and raw emotions are unavoidable speed bumps in life."

Debbie knew the truth in that. She'd been engaged to a wonderful young man over two decades before. He'd been killed while serving overseas, and the heartbreak of what she'd lost had spurred her to stay in Cleveland when school ended. She didn't want to come back to Dennison and face constant reminders of dreams that could never become reality. Cleveland seemed easy by comparison, so she'd found an apartment and worked her way up the corporate ladder.

Her stay there began because of her loss. Then it became more like entrenchment. It continued season by season, goal after goal, year after year, until she finally hit the pause button and realized that life—real life, filled with family and friends—was passing her by. She folded her corporate tent, invested with Janet in a café tucked in one end of the old Dennison train depot, and here she was. Engaged, soon to be married, and surveying a tangled mess of old growth and new sprouts.

"I'm happy to help you with this." Janet slipped her arm through Debbie's. "It looks like a stretch of nice weather starting on Saturday. How about we dive in then? If we focus on one section at a time, I think we can have things shaped up by the beginning of May."

That was a month away. A busy month away. "That long? Really?"

"Sooner, if we work in the evenings too. But it's still chilly once the sun starts to go down. And your schedule is cranking up."

Janet was right. Debbie was just realizing that a spring sports calendar filled quickly when teenagers played on school teams. She and Greg were in the middle of planning a wedding. A big wedding on a short timeline.

She wasn't after the perfect event. But she was hoping for *kind* of perfect, because it *was* her wedding.

Business was good and growing at a rate they'd never expected for year two at the Whistle Stop Café. She wasn't a shrinking violet, and she never shirked a good day's work, but tackling the mess of gardens on top of everything else this month might be foolish. She said as much to Janet, and Janet arched a brow. "Why foolish?"

"It feels like a silly thing to worry about now, with so much else to do. So many decisions to make. I had no idea that planning a wedding involved this many options and meetings. It's not like you just pick this and choose that. It's all about comparison shopping, price points, and even escape clauses."

"You're planning an escape?"

Debbie saw Janet's look of amusement, and rolled her eyes. "Not on a personal level, but if there's a natural disaster or some dreadful illness or something, a good contract will allow you to get out of it."

Janet opened her mouth to reply, but Cecily Markham Haygood's car pulled into the driveway right then. An avid member of the local historical society and garden club, Cecily lived north of Greg's house in a picture-perfect classic colonial. Her two-story home was set back far enough to have a gracious front yard but not so far that her lush gardens weren't ogled and admired by passersby. The strategically curved plantings were symmetrically balanced with a perfect sun-to-shade ratio on the three visible sides of her lovely home. Cecily had explained all this to Debbie. More than once.

Cecily loved Dennison, history, and horticulture. For seven months of the year she worked at the big garden center in New Philadelphia. When it came to pretty yards, Cecily stepped out with a whirlwind of knowledge about everything to do with landscaping on any scale. It was information she avidly shared with anyone who would listen. The last thing Debbie wanted right now was a lecture, but she was afraid she was going to get one.

She had eyes. She saw what a wreck the gardens were, but...

Cecily crossed the driveway briskly. When she paused alongside Debbie, the older woman drew her brows together and pressed her mouth into a tight, thin line. Cecily took a deep breath—and said nothing.

Debbie glanced at Janet then back at Cecily.

Then she greeted Greg's neighbor because that was about the only option left. "Cecily, hello. Nice of you to drop by during such a busy season at the garden center. You're just getting into the crazy time of year up there, aren't you?"

Cecily arched one brow. She did it so well that Debbie was sure she must practice the maneuver in front of a mirror. Then she handed Debbie a flyer. "Our biweekly sales at the center. I know Greg hasn't had time to tend to things, but I also know that's likely to change now that there's going to be a woman in the house."

Debbie accepted the flyer but not the challenge. "This particular woman spent twenty years in a big-city apartment, so I don't pretend to have knowledge of gardens, flowers, bushes, or pretty much anything outside aside from trees. I'm good with trees, which seem to take care of themselves." She aimed a smile at Cecily. "But that's my extent."

Cecily was far too ladylike to show her displeasure. She leaned forward as if sharing a confidence. "And that's why we embrace every opportunity to learn that comes our way. I find women are better at that than men, but I don't say that to too many people, of course. I want you to know I'm available to give advice as needed, even though I'm pretty busy right now with my work and my family. Not to mention my civic duty. I've drawn up a petition to encourage our town leaders to clamp down on people parking monster-sized vehicles in their driveways all year. It's ridiculous and a hazard." She huffed a breath, then changed the subject by directing her gaze to the borders flanking the Connor house. "Anyway, I look for potential. And Debbie Albright-soon-to-be-Connor, there is a wealth of potential surrounding you here. And—"

She stopped talking as Greg's younger son headed their way from the backyard. He carried the family's two garden gnomes, a

boy and a girl. Greg had told her that the boys' mother had purchased the gnomes about ten years before. She'd dubbed them Hans
and Greta, and the beloved pair claimed a spot in the front garden
every year. Julian raised his right hand, the one holding Greta, and
spoke to Debbie. "Dad says supper's about ready and we can put the
gnomes out now. He said the weather is mild enough so they'll
be okay."

"Oh, they're adorable." Janet smiled at Julian. "They're like a little Dutch pair, Julian. Prettier than a lot of gnomes we see around."

"The words *pretty* and *gnome* should never be uttered together."
Cecily sighed. "Although I see more and more of this kind of thing
around town. Gnomes, little signs, metal animals, pinwheels,
wooden flowers. As if God hasn't given us enough natural beauty,
we feel the need to augment His green earth with a hodgepodge of
man-made whatnots. I've a good mind to add banning lawn ornaments to my petition. It's like a springtime invasion that's growing
worse every year."

Julian grinned at her. "But an awesome invasion, right? These
were my mom's." He'd grown this past year. He was taller than Janet
and Debbie, and had Cecily by a good three inches. "She loved
these guys."

"Understandably so." Debbie smiled at her soon-to-be stepson.
"Tuck them in where you'd like them to be, and we'll shift them
around as we clean things up. Okay?"

"Okay." He crossed the yard to place the two small statues on
either side of the front garden plot. "Then I have English homework." The drama in his voice matched the expression on his thirteen-
year-old face. "Book analysis. Why can't she just call it a book report

like every other teacher in the world?" He stood up once the statues were in place.

Janet winked at Debbie as Julian trudged back to the house. She had a college-age daughter and understood teen drama quite well. "I'm heading home to spread mulch. We'll figure this out." She reached out and gave Debbie a half hug. "Promise."

"And my offer of help is evergreen," Cecily said to Debbie. "It's different for artists, you know."

Debbie had no idea what her future neighbor meant.

Never at a loss for words, Cecily was quick to explain. "Artists can paint over a canvas to complete a new work. That option doesn't exist with gardens. Sometimes what they need is a full extraction. Then we begin again. Kind of a metaphor on life, isn't it?" She flashed Debbie a quick smile, then crossed the driveway to her car.

Janet said her goodbye to Debbie then followed Cecily.

Debbie stayed behind, mulling over the weeds, the lack of time, and a to-do list that rivaled any she'd ever dealt with before. But this job felt important, for many reasons.

Julian came out the front door. He clutched a folder and a paperback in his hands. As he took a seat on the steps, two pens tumbled out of the side pocket of his hoodie. They rolled, one after the other, hitting all three steps on their way to the sidewalk below. He let out a woebegone sigh—quite overdone—as he stood to retrieve the pens. Then he sat back down, pulled a sheet of paper from the folder, and set it on his lap.

He frowned as he read, then set the paper down and folded his arms in a move so much like his father's that Debbie felt it inside. "How is anyone supposed to know what this means? Or care? What is Miss McGinnity thinking? 'He was addled with April. He was—'"

"'Dizzy with spring.'" When she saw his surprise, she was pretty sure she'd scored a point with her fiancé's younger son. "Marjorie Kinnan Rawlings. *The Yearling.* Junior high required reading even when I was in school. Mrs. Anderson's class."

He made no attempt to hide his astonishment. "How'd you remember that? It's so random."

"A more apt question is, how could I forget it?" She settled a gardening cushion onto the damp ground. The pad made weeding easier on her clothes and her knees. "One of the best-written coming-of-age books. Right up there with *Where the Red Fern Grows.*"

Julian had solid reading skills. "I liked a lot of books when I was a kid," he told Debbie frankly.

She fought a smile because clearly thirteen was well beyond "kid" stage in Julian's mindset.

"Funny ones, fantasy ones, all kinds of stuff. The Fisher twins were my favorites for a long time, but now I'd rather read books about real-life people who do great things," he continued. "Jackie Robinson. Harriet Tubman. Abe Lincoln. Anyway, I don't know why it has to rain all the time. So many games have been rained out, and we end up having to play a bunch of them all at once. That makes the pitching schedule crazy because you're only allowed so many innings in middle school. I just wanna play baseball."

Today's games had been canceled once again due to wet field conditions, and Greg had asked Julian to give her a hand in the front garden. A break in the rain had offered them a brief window. The rain had softened the soil, making weeding a bit easier, and she and

Julian had tackled a small area when he got home from school, before Janet arrived.

Julian rested his elbow on one knee and propped his chin on his hand, glum.

"I've always liked a book that makes me run the full range of emotions," she told him. She knelt on the pad, ready to start near the sidewalk. "Laugh, cry, mourn. But I expect that rubs salt in the wound when you've lost someone so close to you."

Julian straightened. "You lost someone you loved."

She lifted her gaze to his.

"The guy you were going to marry when you were in college. And you *still* like those books. I don't get it."

"I read them before I'd lost anyone close to me," she replied. "Big difference."

"I guess." He sighed again. "Kelsey is coming over to do this assignment with me."

"Kelsey Addison. Her dad owns the mechanic shop on the far side of town."

"Yeah, and her grandparents own the big farm with all the donkeys."

Debbie knew Claymont Farm well. She and Janet had gone to school with Dani Addison, and they'd recently helped her figure out who was sabotaging their family farm. That hadn't been an easy thing to puzzle out, but they'd persevered. "I love that farm."

"It's cool. They make good doughnuts."

There was an understandable adolescent perspective, but she had to agree. The doughnuts *were* very good. Different from the ones she and Janet served at the café, but there was plenty of room in Dennison for sweet treats.

"Anyway, I don't know why they have to assign homework on weeknights. Or even at all. Or why we have to have partners. But Kelsey knows how to do stuff with a computer that makes the reports look cool."

"Due tomorrow?" she asked.

"Monday."

"That gives you plenty of time," Greg said as he came out the front door. He had a bag slung over his left arm. "There's a problem over at the church. A plumbing mishap. It shouldn't take long. Julian, do you want to come along?"

Julian shook his head. "I've got to get this done."

Debbie stayed quiet.

Greg never forced the boys to help him with his jobs. If they volunteered, that was great, but he wanted their assistance to be on their own terms. She understood his point. And of course schoolwork had to come first.

Jaxon came around the side of the house, shrugging into a lightweight hoodie. "I'll come, Dad."

Greg sent him a grateful look. "Thanks. I could use an extra pair of hands. Pastor Nick has a Bible study tonight, otherwise he'd help me set this straight." He turned back to Debbie. "Don't wait dinner for us. We'll warm it up when we get home."

Julian didn't move until his father and brother had pulled out of the driveway. Then he stood and dusted off the seat of his pants. "I'm going inside. You wanna eat now?"

"I'm not all that hungry yet. I'll come in soon. You said Kelsey was coming over?"

He nodded. "In like an hour."

The poor kid didn't really want to help her, or his father. He wanted to play baseball. Three straight days of rain had thwarted his game and practice schedule that week. "If you want to help me attack this section, we could call it quits in twenty minutes and have supper together," she offered.

He glanced at the gardens bordering the front steps. "I don't think they look too bad. Not really."

"That's code for 'I don't want to get on my hands and knees on the cold, wet ground and pull weeds,' right?" Debbie laughed.

He fought a smile. "Pretty much."

"Go on in. I got this," she told him. He'd been a trouper this afternoon. "Can you go across the front there and straighten Greta? She's tipping."

"Sure." He crossed the grass and lifted the gnome then carefully flattened the ground below before snugging her into place in front of a rosebush.

"Mom wasn't a fan of loading up gardens with goofy things, but she liked these two little gnomes."

"Because they're cute. Like you."

Julian ignored that remark, gave the gnomes one last look, then headed for the house.

An hour later, Amelia Addison swung by with Kelsey. The girl hopped out of the car and started for the house, but paused when Amelia rolled down the passenger window. "Eight o'clock, right? Hey, Debbie, how are you?"

Debbie stood up, her knees protesting the move in spite of the pad she'd set on the ground. She was pretty sure she'd used muscles she hadn't used in a long time, because a fair share of them hurt.

She smiled at Amelia as she rubbed the small of her back. "I'll be better with a mild painkiller and some muscle rub. Hands-and-knees gardening isn't for wimps."

Amelia laughed. "True. I've got plenty to do myself once I find a window of time. So, Kelsey. Eight?" She redirected her attention to her daughter.

Kelsey had politely waited until their conversation paused before answering her mother. "Eight's good. I'm going to show Julian how easy it is to do a report that Miss McGinnity will love so much that she can't help but give it an A." She patted the small bag she had slung over her shoulder and hurried for the side door.

"She's got a techie brain, that one." Amelia watched Kelsey disappear through the door. "Like her dad. Always wondering how to fix this, adjust that, or how things work. I like the actual building of things." Amelia had a finish carpentry business that was doing well.

"Do you want me to drop her off at your house?" offered Debbie. "I'll be heading back to my place about then."

"I'm going to be right up the road at Mom and Dad's, but thank you. I appreciate the offer. Mom's doing up a petition to urge the town to reconsider what people can put in their driveways. It's been a constant discussion since the weather started to break. She's on a mission, and when my mother is on a mission, no one and nothing stands in the way." Amelia grinned. "Good thing she's got a big heart or she'd be unbearable, but she does so much good for everyone she meets that they mostly overlook her bossiness. See you later."

"Yes. And good luck," Debbie teased.

Amelia laughed and backed out of the driveway.

Greg and Jaxon pulled in just as Debbie was leaving to go home. She'd put two bowls of beef stew and the leftovers in the fridge for them and had spent a happy hour with a library book she'd stashed in her purse.

Hammer jumped out of the truck first. The black-and-white border collie loved riding shotgun. He bounded up the steps, paused for a petting, then followed Jaxon through the back door.

Greg gave her a rueful look. "It took longer than expected. I'm sorry. I wanted to spend more of the evening with you."

"Me too. But then there's tomorrow evening. And the next. And the—"

He laughed, caught her up, and spun her around. "And almost every evening after that."

"Yes." She laughed too. "Julian and Kelsey finished the dreaded English assignment, and from the sounds of it they put together a solid report. They have moved on to the Industrial Revolution. I believe they've arrived at an Edison vs. Tesla point in time. They seem to like the drama." She reached up and kissed him. "Come see me at work tomorrow. I'll make you a delicious coffee. Or sandwich. Whatever you'd like."

Greg followed her to her car and opened the door for her. She was about to get in, when she paused.

The dusk-to-dawn lights were all on. The gardens still looked unkempt, so that wasn't what drew her attention.

Still… something looks wrong.

Different. Like there was something missing. Then it hit her. "The gnome."

"What about it?"

"She's gone, Greg. Greta is gone."

He narrowed his gaze. "Probably fell over. I'll check it out." He started crossing the yard toward where Hans still stood, but Debbie caught up to him on the grass.

"She was tipping slightly before we went in," she explained. "Julian fixed her and put her right up against that rosebush, and now she's not there."

He stared at the now-empty spot. "You're sure that's where she was?"

"One hundred percent. She was there when I went inside just over an hour ago." She didn't want to overreact. The little figure was a low-money item but heavy on the emotions. "Where did she go? She's a garden gnome. How did this happen?"

He looked as confused as she felt. "First we need to ask Julian if he moved her. If he didn't, it'll be easier to track her down in the morning." Greg sighed. "An April Fool's joke, maybe?"

"An April Fool's joke that's not one bit funny." Debbie bit her lip, and Greg put his arm around her shoulders.

"Hans is still here. Greta will turn up. She couldn't have gotten too far, right? She *is* mobility challenged." He winked, but Debbie didn't miss the concern in his eyes. The pair of gnomes linked the past with the present. Something of Holly's. A funny, quirky thing the boys remembered. As the years went by, those memories were becoming scarcer, particularly for Julian because he'd been so young when she passed away.

"She could have gotten pretty far if someone stole her."

"Who steals gnomes?" Greg sounded doubtful. "So many people have them. Old ones, fat ones, bearded ones. I'll check with Ian to see if there's some new social media gnome challenge going on. That's the only thing I can think of that could explain something so random and crazy."

For some reason, the missing statue hit Debbie hard. Maybe because she'd been the last one in the yard? "Crazy or not, she's missing. And those gnomes are important to the boys."

"She'll turn up."

She knew she shouldn't worry, but she wasn't born yesterday. The gnome had been there just an hour ago. Now it was gone. Since gnomes couldn't walk, clearly someone took little Greta from her niche in the garden.

Debbie was determined to find out who had that kind of nerve. Even on April Fool's Day.

CHAPTER TWO

"Part of me feels like it's ridiculous to care about a seventeen-dollar garden statue." Debbie made the confession to Janet late the next morning. Paulette, Greg's mom and their part-timer, was watching the front, and Debbie had come into the kitchen to organize the grill area for lunches. "Like I'm overreacting. But I'm not," she added firmly. "Not at all. Because it's not about the value of the gnome."

Janet agreed as she frosted spring-themed cookies. "It never is when it comes to people we love."

"Exactly." Debbie finished restocking the cooler. "It's about the link to their mother." She brought out ham salad and seasoned chicken for lunchtime paninis as she vented.

Debbie had never thought she was reactionary, but she was reacting to this. Big-time. And she was annoyed. "I called Greg this morning to see if they found the statue, and they hadn't. He said he checked all around the yard once the sun came up and there was no sign. But he was able to see the spot Julian hollowed out to stabilize her. The impression was there, in the garden, so he knew what I meant when I said that she didn't just tumble and roll off. So where is she?"

Janet made a face. "It's weird, Debbie. Who would steal a garden gnome in the first place, especially when the family was home? And why take only one when there was a matched set? Boy and girl?"

Debbie had no answer for either question. When Greg stopped by for lunch an hour later, he was just as mystified. "I found nothing," he said when Debbie came out of the kitchen to bring him a grilled-ham-and-cheese with a side of macaroni salad. "I checked the neighbor's doorbell camera, and it caught a car—a small car, kind of grayish-blue. It was getting dark, and she couldn't tell exactly. Anyway, the car stopped just short of our place and stayed there for a minute or two."

"Did someone get out? Or get in?" asked Debbie.

Greg shook his head. "That part of the car was out of range. She saw movement in the upper corner of the feed but couldn't say it was necessarily a person moving. Just a flash."

"Did the boys notice it was gone?"

Greg shrugged one shoulder. "I didn't wait for them to notice. I told them this morning."

"How did they react?"

"Well, considering they're half asleep before school, it didn't hit either one real hard. Jaxon figures it's a prank, and Julian agreed. But he looked worried."

Of course he was. She'd seen his expression the night before as he carried the two statues to the front yard. "He was happy to bring them out and set them in place. It seemed like setting them up is an annual event."

"It kind of is," Greg admitted. "It marks the end of winter. We start a whole new season. Holly made it a mini celebration. She'd get the gardens cleaned out and mulched. Then she'd have the boys bring out the statues. They would each carry one, and she let them set the gnomes wherever they wanted. No matter where they put them, she would tell them it was the perfect spot."

Debbie sighed.

Janet came by with a coffeepot and topped off Greg's mug. "I suppose a replacement is out of the question?" she asked.

Greg didn't look hopeful. "She bought them nearly ten years ago, online. I can do a search, but it's not likely. I'll check it out tonight," he added. Greg placed his hand over Debbie's where it rested on the counter. "It's not the end of the world," he told her.

"I know that. But you told me yourself that the boys were concerned because they felt like they were starting to forget their mother."

He nodded. "And I promised we'd do everything we could to make sure that doesn't happen. I even dug out some more pictures to put around the house. Will that bother you?" He posed the question gently, and Debbie loved him for his concern for her.

"No." She met his gaze, not a scrap of doubt in her mind or her heart. "She gave them life. She should be remembered and loved." Then she leaned forward and kissed his cheek. "I'm not bothered by their love for their mother, but I am intensely irked at the thought of someone stealing a precious memory as if it were meaningless. Did you check with Ian about social media challenges?" Ian, Janet's husband, was Dennison's police chief.

"Yep," Greg replied. "He saw nothing. He even had his daughter check from her devices because she'd be more wired into the right age groups as a nineteen-year-old, and Tiffany didn't find anything in her searches."

"Hmm."

Paulette had been on the dining floor taking orders. She headed their way with two order slips as another pair of customers came through the door.

Debbie gave his hand a light squeeze. "I've got to get back to work. One way or another I'm determined to figure this out," she told him.

Janet came through the swinging door with a wrapped basket of oversized cookies. "*We're* determined." She stressed the pronoun deliberately. "People should be able to put lawn ornaments or garden decor in their yards without worry of thieves. The very thought that widgets and windcatchers and statues might be at risk is crazy. We're going to make sure we find little Greta and return her to her rightful place outside your door."

"Unless the gnome staged a coup due to inhospitable living conditions," offered Debbie. "The garden isn't exactly up to its usual standards."

"In that case, I think she'd surely have taken the love of her life with her." Janet winked at Greg as she set the gift basket at the end of the counter. Her mother was coming by in the next hour to pick up and deliver it to the church. "Let's troubleshoot later. When things calm down."

Janet was right. A busy lunch hour, even with fast-fix menu items, wasn't the time to do a mind-delve, but there was one major difference about this mystery.

It made no sense.

Garden ornaments weren't exactly appealing as a secondhand item for sale. Plus the culprit had only taken one.

Why?

Had it been a neighborhood child, maybe? Drawn to the cute little feminine statue? Maybe the grayish car had nothing to do with the missing ornament.

Debbie pondered options as she wiped down the display case.

She had several after-work appointments scheduled for the coming two weeks. There were cake and food tastings. They needed to decide on a venue for the reception. On top of wedding planning, the boys' schedules had increased massively because of last month's canceled baseball games. That meant their April schedule was already teeming, not to mention Holy Week and Easter.

She seated two more tables.

The church for the wedding was a no-brainer. They were both members of Faith Community, but that was where simple came to a dead stop. Greg wanted to help, but he'd contracted home improvement and renovation jobs well into the following winter, so his time was restricted too.

Janet came through the swinging door. She grabbed a small to-go container and handed it to Debbie. "Paulette and I can handle this for a while. You go get Greg, and take this with you," she added, handing off the container.

Debbie glanced from the to-go box to Janet. "Why?"

"Because Ian just texted that other lawn ornaments are missing from various parts of town. An old chipped bench that looked worse for wear, according to its owner, and a small shepherd's hook from another spot. According to the owner it had a flag on it, and that's gone too."

Debbie stared at her. "More? Is Ian at the police station?"

The Dennison police department was housed in a vintage building on Grant Street, the main drag running through their pretty little town. The town center had undergone a thorough renovation the past year. New pavers and benches, vintage streetlights, hanging baskets, flags, and gorgeous planters had given their business district the kind of inviting look that made a small town come alive.

"Yes. He'd come over, but they're doing some photo shoots of all the town's new improvements, and they want him for some of the photos. They're going to use them on the town's website and on social media platforms. Go see him. See what he has to say."

"We will." As soon as she got to where Greg was seated at the counter, she realized they wouldn't need the container after all. He had only a handful of fries remaining, and they were disappearing at a rapid rate. She tucked the container on the shelf running beneath the counter and took Greg's empty plate. "Hungry, huh?"

"That and the café having the best food ever." He grinned at her. "Ian texted me."

"So Janet said. Let's head up the street and see what's going on. I can't even imagine what someone's motive would be. Do you have a few minutes?"

He sent a quick text and flashed her a smile. "I do now. I'm doing a project for Bernice Byrne. I told her I might be running a little behind. She's a bit eccentric, but she's a stickler for getting things done right. When she remembers, that is."

They hurried through the depot museum's ticketing and waiting area. When they got to the door leading to Center Street, Greg opened it for her. Once outside, he reached over and took her hand in his. "Weird things happen in every town. Think of all the mysteries you and Janet have solved."

She squeezed his hand. "I know. This isn't just about us or a couple of missing low-end items. It's about the boys' feelings and how somebody thought it was okay to take something that didn't belong to them. Something irreplaceable, because even if we found a similar girl gnome, it wouldn't be the one Holly bought. That makes all the difference."

He let go of her hand, slid his arm around her shoulders, and kissed her temple. "It sure does, honey. It sure does."

CHAPTER THREE

ot your usual case, for sure." Ian had opted for his casual uniform style for the town's photo op in the Village Hall. Debbie had only seen him wear his dress uniform at formal occasions. His calm, man-of-the-people air endeared him to others, and his ability to get things done kept him in his job. "A garden flag, your gnome, two others that had seen better days, a trio of leprechauns, a bench, and a shepherd's hook." He drew his brows down as he shared the images with Debbie and Greg. "What would someone do with a mishmash like this? And why?"

"It makes no sense." Debbie looked from Ian to Greg. "Where were the other things taken from? Also on Greg's street?"

Ian shook his head. "No. One incident was from Silas Thumm's yard, over near McCluskey Park—"

"But that's a tight neighborhood," Greg interrupted. "The houses are pretty close together. No one saw anything?"

"Not that we've ascertained, but then the reports just came in this morning. An accident on the highway took precedence."

"Sorry. Of course it did. And I know—we know"—Greg included Debbie with a look—"that garden decorations are probably a low-priority kind of thing. But it's become more of a brainteaser with other things going missing. Where was the third theft?"

"Rose Hill Orchard," Ian replied.

Debbie knew exactly where that was. Just north of Claymont Creek Farm, owned by Kelsey Addison's grandparents, where she and Janet had tracked down the miscreant who'd been making trouble for the third-generation farm. Debbie had heard that Rose Hill had recently been sold.

"That's such a pretty place."

"It sure is," Ian responded. "The new owners put the garden flag out last week. They set it next to that hand-carved 'Rose Hill Orchard' sign, so the flag was pretty close to the road. That made it an easy target. Then the leprechaun decorations were in Chip Calloway's side yard, left over from March. He said he usually puts them away at the end of the month and didn't get around to it yet."

"No doorbell camera at Rose Hill or the Calloway place?" Greg asked.

Ian drummed his fingers on the table. "Cameras on the house wouldn't be Chip's style. The new people said our low crime rate and great neighborhoods drew them to buy near Dennison and that the theft surprised them because our town is such a friendly place."

"It is," Debbie said. "You know what?" She faced both men.

"What?" Greg lifted an eyebrow.

"It's spring. Kids do weird things in the spring after being cooped up half the winter. Even if it's not one of those crazy social media things, I'm going to assume it's some teenage prank and hope they have the decency to return the items. Or at least put them in the donation bin outside the thrift store. We can let Margie Kendrick know what to look for. If they show up in her donation bin, she can contact the owners."

Margie Kendrick ran a vintage resale shop not far from the depot. Her parents had owned the building for decades, but when the storefront remained empty for a few years, Margie took it on herself to establish a thrift store, long before "thrifting" became a thing. Now she ran a flourishing business, especially when kids were home on college breaks. At the end of each season Margie would donate a share of her proceeds to the local food shelf.

"You know, that's not a bad idea." Ian rubbed his jaw. "If we post on our social media page that items can be returned to the thrift store, that might coax the bandit to give them back. I think Margie would go along with that."

"I can stop in and see her," offered Debbie.

Mayor Allarico called Ian's name. Picture time.

Ian answered Debbie before joining the group near the Village Hall entrance. "That would be great. I'll have the mayor post the info when we're finished with pictures. He's devoted to seeing this town thrive again. He won't like that someone is messing with our Good Neighbor policy."

"Great," Greg said as his phone buzzed.

"That's probably Bernice," Debbie told him. "I don't want you to keep her waiting. I know you need to get over there."

She turned and gave Ian a gentle chuck on the arm. "Thanks, buddy. You know we appreciate the help."

"No problem." Ian winked at them as two women came through the Grant Street door. They'd been talking together but paused to let Ian cross the room.

Alicia Whitman was the woman closest to Greg and Debbie. She offered Ian a warm greeting. Then she gave a quick smile and nod to Greg as she and her companion moved deeper into the town offices.

Nothing for Debbie. Alicia moved on by, as if dismissing Debbie's significance at Greg's side.

Greg nodded back, but now he was busy typing on his phone. Debbie felt the slight because it wasn't the first time Holly's old friend had snubbed her.

So far she'd shrugged it all off. Least said, soonest mended. They rarely saw one another, so it wasn't a major problem, but it had been becoming more frequent. Should she mention it to Greg?

A part of her said yes. Another part—the calmer part—advised patience. She decided to heed her own advice.

Ian had caught up with the other town leaders for the photo op. Jim Watson was there, hobnobbing with the fire chief, the council members, the mayor, and a couple of local business owners.

Jim Watson ran the *Gazette*, their local weekly paper. He had organized a series of articles showing village improvements over the last ten years. As the physical changes were wrapping up, he wanted to bring the readers up to date on what was happening next. The weekly offering might be one of the few remaining newspapers to see readership numbers trending up, and that was because of Jim. Residents respected their local newsman, and they loved the *Gazette*.

Debbie said a quick goodbye to Greg when they got to his truck, then hurried back to the café.

A school field trip to the adjacent railroad museum had the café humming. Parents grabbed coffees, and the kids, a group of middle schoolers from New Philadelphia, picked up cupcakes and cookies before reboarding their buses.

By the time things quieted down around one thirty, there was plenty of clean-up to do.

"I'm mopping today. With bleach," Paulette announced as she stacked chairs into two separate corners. "That higher sun invites every ant there is to come up through the dirt and stretch their legs. Those sugar ants will hightail it to these crumbs as soon as they smell them."

"I fight them every spring, all along my kitchen counter," Janet added. "We even have the outside perimeters treated now, like Kim does here, but those little ones find their way in. You can almost read the calendar by their punctuality."

"I'll take kitchen duty." Debbie propped the swinging door open as she went through. She took a moment to answer the phone when Greg's name popped up in her display. "Hey, future husband. Are you all set at Bernice's place?"

"No." He was talking softly. Very softly. She hiked up the volume on her phone to hear him.

"I'm on my way to my truck," he told her. "I've got to go get a few things to take care of the problems here, so I'm heading to the hardware store. But I noticed something odd. Maybe not odd," he corrected himself. "Maybe it's just her way of doing things, but Bernice has a whole slew of yard things in her garage. Not a normal amount by any standard. Even hers."

Bernice Byrne came into the café occasionally. Her age remained a mystery. According to Janice, she could be anywhere from seventy to ninety. No one really knew, and Bernice wasn't one to tell. In the end, it didn't matter. Other than some memory issues that had plagued her for decades, Bernice was fine to live life on her own, saving cats.

Lots of cats.

She'd found a veterinarian who would spay and neuter them for her at a reduced rate. Then she would find the cat a home.

She was the oxymoron of a typical cat lover because, as far as Debbie knew, she had no cat of her own. She simply saved them, fixed them up, and gave them to other people. Her shaky memory had seemed worse than usual the last few times she'd been in, but harsh winters were sometimes rough, on both young and old.

"I haven't been out to her place since I moved back," Debbie said. "But a lot of people love to decorate their yards in the nicer months. Ray used to make all kinds of things in the garage before he moved to Good Shepherd." Ray Zink had owned Debbie's house before he went into assisted living a couple of years before. "I remember Mom saying they sold his woodworking equipment at the auction before I bought the house, but she made sure to buy a few of his creations for their place and mine before they sold out."

Buying Ray's house was how she'd first met Greg. She'd contracted him to renovate her basement, and he'd done a great job on that project. They'd discovered a mutual appreciation for history and the famous depot and somehow managed to fall in love along the way.

"I'm not talking a reasonable amount here." She heard the truck door close. Once it did, Greg began speaking in a more normal tone. "We're talking one whole side of her big garage filled with yard stuff. She doesn't have much on display in her yard, just a few things here and there. Not that her lot is big enough for a quarter of it, unless she turns the old carriage house into a display area. Maybe that's what she's got in mind. And remember? She drives a little gray Chevy."

Like the one that had been seen in Greg's neighborhood the night of the theft. Debbie swallowed hard. "Did you look at the stuff in the garage? Look through it?"

"No. But if I have another chance to peek in and it's not outright snooping through her belongings, I will. I recognized a few things you see in lots of yards. Flags, metal flowers, and some bigger things. A wooden wagon, a small wishing well. All things that looked like they could use a little love."

Debbie's heart sank.

Not because Bernice might have nipped things here or there—although there was no proof yet that she had done so—but because she'd been able to live an independent life up to this point. How much longer could that go on if she was, in fact, stealing things from people's yards?

"I'll see what, if anything, I can find out when I get back here tomorrow," he promised. "Right now I need to head over to my mom's place to replace that bad weather stripping on her back door. Then I'll grab the boys from baseball practice."

"Paulette is still here, so she may not be there when you arrive. I'm going to stop by the thrift store on my way home. Janet made bread dough this afternoon and bagged me up a piece for home-made pizza tonight. Sound good?"

"Pizza always sounds good. I'll see you at home."

"You sure will."

Home.

She'd thought it would be odd to call Greg's house "home" after buying her own place. Fixing things up. Adding this and adding that.

It wasn't as odd as she'd thought.

The boys had lived in that Cape Cod all their lives. They had friends nearby, and the empty field across the road gave all the neighborhood kids a place to play a game of pickup baseball or soccer or football. Greg kept it mowed. It was like having a personal park right there.

They'd agreed that the boys shouldn't be moved after the wedding, but she did wonder if her presence in their home, in Greg's life, would mess with their peace of mind. They liked her now, she knew that. But they were still kids. Would that be enough?

Janet came through the door. She gave the still messy kitchen a puzzled look. "Didn't get too far, eh?" She laughed.

Debbie tucked the phone into her pocket. "Sideswiped by love."

Janet put a hand to her heart. "Never let it be said I'd get in the way of true love." She crossed to the far side of the small kitchen. "I'll do the back counters. You do the grill. Then we can do the floor, because Paulette's right. Ants do love crumbs, and my baking area is like an open invitation."

Paulette gave them a quick wave from the door. "If you two have this, I'm heading out to meet Greg. The front floor will be dry in a few minutes."

"Thank you, Paulette!" Debbie waved her grill scraper in salute. "See you tomorrow. Unless you want to come over for pizza tonight. There'll be plenty."

Paulette's smile made Debbie glad she'd issued the invitation. "I'd love that, actually. Is six good?"

"It sure is."

"I'll be there!" Greg's mother promised, and then she hurried out.

Once she'd gone, Debbie filled Janet in on what Ian had told them a few hours before. She ended with what Greg had revealed about Bernice's garage.

Janet bit her lip as she finished wiping down the baking counters. "Bernice has always been quirky, but as far as I know she's never been a hoarder. She's hosted the ladies' sewing group from Sadie Flaherty's doll shop, and they've made all kinds of cute things, including all those quilted lap throws for residents at Good Shepherd. I've never been to her home, but I'm pretty sure we'd have heard if hoarding was a problem. The fire chief's wife is one of the quilting ladies, and you know the chief takes safety to heart. He's a gentle soul, but he'd have gone to see her and offer help like he's done in other situations with unsafe fire conditions. Did she have other things in the garage? Or just yard stuff?" she asked.

Debbie shrugged. "I don't know. Greg said the amount of yard decor was over-the-top." She filled Janet in on her plan to talk to Margie at the thrift shop.

"That's an excellent idea." Janet finished washing down the counter while Debbie tied off the garbage bag for the dumpster out back. "Mind if I tag along?"

"Are you kidding? Let's go."

"Good. I'm planning out my Holy Week and Easter baking schedule tonight, so Ian's bringing home take-out. A few minutes' walk to see Margie will be wonderful. That sunshine's been calling to me all day."

"A long, wet March will do that to you." Debbie locked the door once they were outside. They turned left, heading for Thrift &

Threads on North First Street, but Harry Franklin and his dog Crosby met up with them at the corner of Third and Center.

"Ladies!" The elderly gentleman offered them a broad smile as they drew close. "That French toast has stuck by me all day. I love having your little café practically in my backyard."

Crosby, who had enjoyed an egg this morning while Harry had breakfast, gazed up at his ninety-plus-year-old owner as if appreciating his love and generosity.

Harry was a regular at the café. He'd worked in multiple capacities at the depot since before America joined the Second World War, and if there were four things Harry Franklin loved, they were God, his family, his dog, and the Dennison Depot.

"You ladies have a nice walk, you hear? A good walk on a fine day is something to be thankful for," he said. "And I am thankful, although I had a bit of a surprise this morning when I got back home. Not a pleasant one at that."

Debbie registered the note of angst in Harry's voice. "What happened? Something you need fixed, Harry? We can call Greg. Or is it something we can help with?"

"Nothing like that," Harry said. "Patricia gave me a call because that old wooden sign disappeared off her porch. The one I gave my wife nearly thirty years back, a part of First Corinthians 13. We used that verse at our wedding, and it meant a lot to my missus. We passed the sign on to our daughter and then to our sweet Patricia when Sylvia was fading away on her trip home to Jesus. It went missing today. Now who would do a thing like that?"

Debbie exchanged a look with Janet.

Patricia was Harry's granddaughter, a successful Dennison attorney. She lived on the upper end of town in a lovely neighborhood not far from McCluskey Park. That made two different homes in the park neighborhood that had been targeted. But by whom? And why? Not one thing taken was of anything more than minor value.

On the surface, a handful of little things going missing wouldn't seem important to most people, but Debbie knew better.

The Connors' gnome and now Harry's sign weren't simply casual yard decor, set out when winter storms had drawn to a close. They were irreplaceable parts of their personal histories. One way or another, Debbie was going to find out who was behind these thefts and stop them.

CHAPTER FOUR

hrift & Threads was tucked away on First Street, between Grant and Center Street. Margie excelled at decorating the shop front for every season, including the posts supporting the simple overhang that protected incoming customers from rain. The overhang also sheltered the shop's sidewalk displays from direct sun. Her nod to spring included bright wooden tulips tacked to the wall and posts, daffodils and pinwheels marking the small grassy areas flanking the sidewalk, and some charming painted bunnies. The storefront was awash in spring-themed pastels, and the window decals on the multipaned door showcased baby birds, kittens, puppies, and a blanket-carrying stork.

An antique bell jangled their arrival as they entered, and Margie looked up from a nearby display. "Janet, Debbie! How nice to see you." She hurried their way, smiling, but then Margie Kendrick was rarely without a smile. "Isn't this just a marvelous day?"

Debbie laughed. "That is the town consensus, Margie. I don't know anyone down South who appreciates a sunny day more than we Northerners when spring finally appears."

"Did you notice that last little window decal on the upper pane of the door?" Marjorie positively beamed.

Janet lifted both brows as she raised her gaze to the upper windowpanes. "Baby on board?" she asked.

"My oldest daughter's due date is next week, and we are *so* excited," she told them. "Of course, she lives an hour away, but an hour isn't all that much for a grandma with a goal, is it?"

Debbie smiled in agreement. "I expect not. Are you closing up while you're gone?"

Margie shook her head. "No. Sadie Flaherty's daughter is going to keep the shop open in the afternoons. She's out of school by one this semester, and that girl's got a good head on her shoulders. Great personality too. She's got a busy soccer schedule, but that's in the evening and we're closed by six until next month. Are you ladies looking for anything in particular?"

"Help," said Debbie. Then she explained what was going on.

Margie offered them a look of commiseration. "The mayor called me. Bud wanted to make sure I'd be okay with using our bin as a drop-off, and I said it was fine." She pointed toward the window. Outside, a large, covered bin was visible on the driveway side of the building. "It's not a bad place if someone wants to avoid trouble. This is a discreet spot after dark. The streetlight is far enough away that if someone wanted to quietly return what they'd taken, they'd be able to do it easily and anonymously enough."

She was correct. Her business faced a municipal parking lot that was generally empty at night unless there was a town event happening, and there weren't any of those scheduled in the next few weeks, to Debbie's knowledge.

"Tucker Lewis came by too."

Tucker and the mayor ran the town's active social media sites.

"He thinks it's likely a teenager messing around. But not too many teens are following our town's social media feeds, I'd venture to guess," she added. "Adults, yes. Business owners, absolutely. But I do know that Bud Allarico and Tucker linked one site to another so his posts reach even more people now. That'll help."

"Bud's been an amazing mayor, and I love how he's taken this town to heart," noted Janet. "Between him and Tucker, our social media is kept up to date and they're always posting local business shout-outs. That's huge in a small town."

"A couple of great guys," agreed Debbie. "I hope the posts will make a difference. I know our little gnome has no monetary value, but the boys' mother bought her when they were small, and that sentimental value means a lot."

"It sure does. I'll be on the lookout," Margie promised. "And Janet, I'm going to call in an Easter order for Holy Saturday, all right? We should have the baby here by then. I don't want to spend time baking when I could be spending time cuddling a new granddaughter. Look what Abby Meyers sent up from Florida when she heard." She held up her phone. The display featured an image of an intricately quilted baby blanket. The background was pieced in shades of pink and rose, and each square featured a beautiful flower.

Abby was a skilled quilter who wintered in Florida and spent summers living with her daughter, helping run a local fabric and notions shop. "Oh, that's precious!" Debbie smiled broadly as she took the phone for a closer look. "She went full-on pink, didn't she?"

"Intentionally," Margie replied. "She sent a lovely note along and told Candace that this wasn't designed to be passed down to a little brother someday. She said she'd make a new one for any siblings that might come along. Abby's reasoning was that every child deserves something made just for them. She also said pink would work best for this baby if she turned out to be as bald as Candace was."

Janet laughed. "I remember Candace being bald. They didn't have as many cute hats and headbands for baby girls back then. Everyone thought she was a boy."

Margie sighed. "They sure did. She was almost two before she had enough hair for me to get a bow to stay put. I think I drowned her in pink and ruffles to give people a clue, and some of them still got it wrong."

"Well, the blanket is beautiful." Debbie handed Margie's phone back to her. "A new family heirloom."

"Candace loves it."

Janet pointed to a sales rack facing the front window. A gray sweatshirt, boldly labeled *Case Tech*, was hanging in a place of honor on a raised bar. "Is that really a vintage Case Western University sweatshirt?"

Margie nodded. "Sure is. Before Tech merged with Western Reserve to form the new school. One of our new neighbors is an alumnus, and he brought in several things."

"I'm grabbing that for Tiffany." She handed it to Margie to ring up the sale. "She loves these vintage looks." Janet took the sweatshirt off the display and gave an appreciative sigh. "This has got to be at least sixty years old and looks almost unused."

"He said he got it as a gift right before the schools merged decades ago." Margie took the sweatshirt, folded it neatly, and settled it into a paper bag. "Is Tiffany coming home this summer?"

"She is." Janet took the bag and tucked it under her arm. "She's working as a lifeguard again. She loves the water, and she's got a great attention span. And of course we're always happy to have her home for a while. We're accustomed to having her away at school but we both love it when she's back home. Even if we barely see her between work and friends. There's something tangible about how kids fill up the empty spaces of a house."

"I cried every time I dropped a kid off at college." Margie made the confession with a sympathetic smile. "My husband would just shake his head, but I made sure I had tissues handy. I hear you."

Janet raised the bag on her arm. "Thanks, Margie. I'm glad I spotted this."

"And I'll keep a watch on the bin," Margie promised.

The warmth of the day still welcomed them when Debbie and Janet stepped outside. "It's been a long time since we had an afternoon walk that wasn't bothered by wind or rain or clouds," Debbie said.

"I know," Janet replied. "I love it. Now we get to turn our attention to a summertime wedding. It will be beautiful."

"More beautiful if I actually firm up choices," Debbie lamented. "I'm a frugal person with simple tastes."

"Me too," Janet agreed as they walked. "That's why we work so well together."

"I get sticker shock every time I get a quote for anything to do with this wedding." Debbie hated to make the confession, but it was the beginning of April and she and Greg were hoping to be married mid-July. That wasn't going to happen if she didn't start setting a plan in motion. "I'm no miser, and I want a nice wedding, but I hesitate every time I go to commit to anything other than the church. I have to stop doing that or everything will be booked up. The caterer, the flowers, the music. Don't even get me started on the dress."

"I thought we were going to look for that on Monday? You, me, Paulette, your mom, and my mom. Right after work."

"That was the plan, but another one of Julian's games was canceled, and it's rescheduled for that afternoon. So do I miss his game to go dress shopping?"

Janet didn't hesitate. "Yes," she told her. "One hundred times yes. This isn't just any old dress." She met Debbie's gaze head-on. "It's a wedding gown. *Your* wedding gown. Julian will understand. And just so you know, no parent gets to be at everything. We all miss something. Greg will be there. You'll be at all their games this week, right?"

"Absolutely."

"Then you can put the guilt card right back into the deck," Janet advised.

Debbie swallowed a sigh. "I know you're right."

Janet grinned. "I never tire of hearing that."

Debbie grinned back. "I need to start making some firm decisions. My mother reminds me regularly," she continued. "Not in a bad way, but the nudges are there. Paulette keeps offering to help, but I feel like I'm drifting."

Janet slowed her steps. "Drifting how?"

Debbie wasn't sure herself, but she tried to explain anyway. "We have a boy that may be going off to college in two years. Then Julian will follow two years later. Those can be mind-boggling financial figures these days. I've been so careful with money all my life, and the thought of tens of thousands of dollars streaming out over the next few years gives me chills. Which is ridiculous, because Greg has money put away for the boys. Some from work and some from Holly's insurance, so a good share of their education can be paid out of that, depending on where they decide to go."

She drew a deep breath, then continued. "Greg says we can have whatever kind of wedding I want. My parents want to help fund the wedding, but with them being at retirement age, I feel dreadful having them spend money on this. We're pooling our resources, but I look at five grand here, four grand there, and seven thousand to feed guests a fairly basic meal, and my stomach ties up in a knot." She sighed. "I love the idea of a nice wedding, but I hate the thought of spending all that money on a day. It makes no sense to me."

Janet slipped her free arm through Debbie's. "Weddings don't have to be big and grand to be wonderful. Some of the best ones I've seen have been smaller, more private affairs."

"Logic agrees," Debbie told her. "I've spent my adult life planning, doing, and overseeing a great group of employees in Cleveland, so why am I having so much trouble with something this special? This important? It doesn't make sense."

"Maybe because it *is* this special. This important. Business is business," Janet reminded her as they drew close to their parked cars. "Personal is different. Weddings aren't your everyday casual affair. And gaining a whole new family will be an adjustment for all of you. Do you want help?"

Debbie almost said yes. Then she paused. "Give me a few more days. It's not that all of you haven't offered help. It's more that I don't need witnesses to my indecisiveness."

"Debbie. Friend." Janet gave her a hug that Debbie sorely needed. "You've never liked being in new water. You like knowns. You've been that way all your life, but since a wedding is a once-in-a-life-time event, it's uncharted territory and that's not comfortable for you. You're making too much of the whole thing."

"But—"

"It's a wedding, yes. But that day isn't the important part. The lifetime after is what matters. That's where your focus should be."

Janet was right.

Absolutely right.

Debbie headed home, determined to follow her friend's advice.

CHAPTER FIVE

A half hour later she'd showered and changed into baseball friendly clothes, including a Claymont High School sweatshirt. Paulette was proud to wear one she'd acquired a quarter century before, when Greg played for Claymont. That old jacket showed wear along the elbows, collar, and sleeves, but Paulette beamed every time she wore it to one of the boys' games, like she was wearing her heart on her sleeve for Greg and her two grandsons.

Debbie wanted to do the same.

She arrived at the field midway through the first inning. Greg was standing at the base of the bleachers. He caught sight of her, came her way, and wrapped her in a big, warm hug. Then he stepped back and shot the hooded sweatshirt an approving look. "Love your team spirit."

She laughed. "Who knew they had high school fan sites online?" She saw Julian sitting up top with Paulette. "I'm going to head up there and cheer with your mom. I'm sure Julian wants to go sit with his friends. You coming?"

"I'll be up shortly. I was waiting for you, and now I see one of my clients trying to get my attention. Be right back." He strode off. She hoped his client wasn't the overly talkative type so Greg could get back to the game soon.

Debbie was about to step up onto the bleachers when Ashling Kelly came her way. Ashling caught Debbie's attention with a quick wave, then motioned her to a small alcove beyond the bleachers, alongside the center stairs.

Ashling was a good friend of Janet's daughter, Tiffany, who was away at college. Ashling had stayed close to home after high school and was now running a Girl Scout troop that met regularly at Faith Community Church. She had a good heart.

Ashling glanced around the alcove before bringing her bright green eyes back to Debbie. She leaned in close and whispered, "I heard about the Connors' gnome going missing."

Debbie didn't try to hide her surprise. "How?"

"Kids sharing stuff on social media. Someone heard it from one of Greg's boys—Julian, I think. Then it got shared all over the school and the town. I think kids thought it was funny or weird or something and worth sharing. Anyway…" She took a slight pause, then spoke, still whispering. "I might know who took it."

"Really?" Debbie's heart skipped a beat. This could be a solid lead. "How would you know that?"

"We had a troop meeting right after school today."

There wasn't anything unusual about that. The troop met every Wednesday afternoon.

Ashling continued, "I heard Alicia Whitman talking to one of the other moms." She hesitated. "She wasn't being very nice."

Alicia again.

Was it a coincidence that her name came up now? Was Debbie's engagement to Greg pushing her over some unseen edge? Instigating negative reactions?

According to Greg, Alicia had been the maid of honor at Greg and Holly's wedding eighteen years before. She'd stayed close with Holly through thick and thin and had been a wonderful help to Greg and the boys in the two years following Holly's death. As time went on they'd seen less of her. Lately, since Debbie and Greg's engagement had become public knowledge, Alicia had been cool and dismissive anytime Debbie had encountered her. Her disregard made Debbie feel awkward, but she'd ignored it so far because she'd done nothing wrong. Ashling wasn't a gossip, in Debbie's experience, so for her to reach out meant the young woman was genuinely concerned. "What was she being not nice about?"

Ashling took a deep breath. "You."

Debbie bit back a sigh. She wanted to be candid with Ashling but didn't want to fuel the fire. It didn't take much to spread gossip in a small town, even a close-knit one like theirs. Just like the gnome story. "I think she's just having a hard time with me stepping into Holly's spot with the Connor guys. Even though it's been a long time. I say we shake it off."

"My grandma said the same thing," Ashling replied. "Except when I told her what happened, she said I should share it with you. And just you."

Those words upped the ante somewhat. "Something happened?"

"She told one of the moms that she was tempted to go over to Greg's and take out everything that had been Holly's because they shouldn't be left there for some new woman to come in and pack it all away."

Debbie frowned. "She said those words?"

"Yes, and I hate telling you that. You've been so nice to me and Tiffany. You let me bring the troop to the café and earn their business badge. It's important for the girls to see successful women in every walk of life."

Debbie hid her amusement. Ashling was legally an adult but still only a few years older than some of her "girls." She thought back to the troop's visit. "Alicia wasn't here for that, was she?"

"She said she couldn't make it, but now I wonder if she did that deliberately to avoid you. She didn't say as much, but hearing her talk I'm also wondering if she's mad enough or sad enough to try and mess things up for you. Doing stuff like that would be wrong. Really wrong."

"You're right. Although she might have been blowing off steam. I think we should leave it at that. She doesn't know me. We've only met casually a couple of times, and maybe it's hard for her to see me with Greg and the boys. Let's cut her some slack."

"I will." Ashling's expression offered understanding, but her eyes darkened. "But Grandma and I thought you should be told about it. With the gnome going missing like that."

"Except if I'm her motivation, she'd have no reason to take things from other people, right?"

"Grandma said the same, but then she said it didn't mean that all those things are related. Maybe it's not the same person who took the other stuff. Grandma liked Holly a lot, but she said Alicia can be the kind of person that you like from a distance."

Debbie had known a few people like that over the years. "I hear you. Thank you, Ashling." Ashling hurried back to her seat on the far side of the bleachers. Debbie paused a moment before joining Paulette and Greg, who must have finished speaking with his client, because he was now in place next to his mother.

She'd spent two decades working in a large Cleveland office. She'd worked her way up the ladder, so she wasn't unaware of the drama people caused or embraced along the way. A chance to escape that was one of the things that had brought her back to Dennison. Yet here it was, rearing its head in her little hometown.

Unless it was on a stage, with a set and actors, she didn't like drama.

The missing garden statue probably had nothing to do with Alicia Whitman, but Ashling's grandmother was right about one thing. Some people were better kept at a distance, and Alicia might fit that category quite well.

The next morning, Debbie brought a small notebook to work. On one page she'd jotted down a list of things to do for the wedding.

The next pages held thoughts and ideas about the missing yard ornaments.

Janet lifted both brows when Debbie handed her the notepad. "Clearly you have your priorities straight."

Debbie didn't miss a beat. "Making these wedding decisions will be easier now that I have a list to work from. Things going missing from people's yards throughout town is a little more difficult to figure out. But most important right now, don't mess up those lemon bars." She aimed a look of caution at the bakery table. "They smell amazing."

"A spring favorite." Janet slipped two big trays into the oven, set her phone timer, then studied the notebook. Her look of interest deepened when she read Debbie's notes about Alicia Whitman. "How do you know this about Alicia?"

"Ashling overheard her talking at the Scout meeting yesterday. She filled me in at Jaxon's baseball game."

"Oh, man." Janet frowned. "I can't believe she'd do something that could deliberately hurt the boys' feelings, but I can totally hear her saying these words. She didn't used to be so negative. I think that's why Greg eased away from that friendship after Holly was gone. She was kind of intrusive, and Greg's the kind of guy that keeps things close to his chest."

"True."

"But taking the statue?" Janet frowned. "That seems out of character and too risky. It's not like she could display it, and her kids would know it was the Connors' statue because they've been to their house over the years. But why be nasty about you? She doesn't even know you."

Debbie had been thinking about that too. "Maybe some people don't react well when they think they're being replaced. Or people they love are being replaced. I don't think it's all that unnatural."

Janet disagreed. "I don't find it natural at all. I think everyone should mind their own business and celebrate others' happiness. Yours and Greg's. But then, I'm an optimist. I like to recognize the good in people. It's there, even if we have to dig a little deeper with some."

"That's not an issue with our first customers of the day." Debbie slipped the notepad into her pocket and aimed a broad smile at Harry and Crosby as they came through the door. "Good to see you, gentlemen! What can we get you on this fine spring morning?"

Harry matched her smile. "I'm of a mind to go off the beaten path today, Debbie."

She leaned forward, interested. "Do tell."

He laughed softly as Crosby settled at his feet. "Drizzle's coming in and lasting for a couple of days, so it feels like oatmeal will be the ticket. I'll have a bowl with brown sugar, walnuts, and raisins, and a hot cup of joe. Plus one slice of wheat toast."

"And the usual for our four-legged friend here?" Debbie shifted her smile down to Crosby. The dog had a wonderful history, not unlike his owner. An ancestry that stretched back to the First World War and the brave men and women who fought for freedom.

"Yes, ma'am. An egg, please. He's got no great love for oatmeal."

Debbie exchanged a knowing look with the elderly gentleman. "I believe it."

She'd just delivered Harry's bowl of steaming hot cereal when his granddaughter strolled into the café. Patricia Franklin had made it a point to come into the café just about every morning since they opened nearly two years before. She had a knack for making her drop-ins seem natural, ostensibly for a peppermint mocha and something delicious out of Janet's bakery display case.

Both Debbie and Janet knew better. The successful local attorney liked to check up on her elderly grandfather without looking like she was checking up on him, and she did it well.

"Pop Pop!"

Harry did nothing to hide his delight when he heard her come in. He turned quickly on the spinning stool. "There's my girl," he declared. There was no mistaking the pride in his voice. He patted the spot beside him. "Come sit by me a minute. You're just the person I wanted to see."

Patricia settled into the seat alongside Harry. "What's up?"

"That sign of your grandmother's," he told her.

Debbie's ears perked up.

Harry set down his spoon and frowned. "I don't know what to make of it being taken, and I don't know why that fancy doorbell of yours didn't get a picture of this person. They had to come up on your porch to get it, didn't they?"

Patricia shook her head. "They didn't, I'm sorry to say. I used the nice weekend weather to give the porch a well-deserved cleaning after a long winter. Then I took the sign, attached it to a yard stake I had in my shed, and put it out front. You know how Nana loved her flowers?"

Harry dipped his chin in agreement. "She sure did."

"Well, there's a nice spray of jonquils and tulips out front of my place right now. I placed the sign in behind the flowers. 'Love is patient…'" she began.

"'Love is kind.'" Harry sighed. "That was your grandmother, all right."

"The camera picked up nothing more than a gray car going by under the streetlight."

A gray car. Again. But Debbie didn't let herself get too excited, because gray and silver were popular vehicle colors. Dennison's parking lots and driveways were filled with them.

She hated to leave the conversation, but she needed to check on other customers and to see if Janet needed help. As if on cue, Janet stuck her head around the corner. "I've got everything under control," she told Debbie. Then she indicated Patricia and Harry with a slight tilt of her head. "You go ahead and visit for a while."

"I will." She sent Janet a quick smile of understanding. "Thank you."

Harry and Patricia were still talking about the car. "Did it just pull up and someone stole the sign out of the ground?" wondered Harry.

Patricia shook her head. "The car went right on by, Pop Pop. But there is a slight movement in the upper corner of the camera's range not long after that. Just a few seconds. Then nothing. So maybe that's when it went missing. But maybe not. It's not proof of anything."

Harry looked distressed, but Patricia eased that by slipping her arm around his shoulders.

"Not to worry," Patricia told him. "If it doesn't turn up soon, I'm going to have someone at the craft co-op out at Hummingbird Acres make me a new one. I've got pictures of the sign. There's a vendor at the barn who does beautiful work with wood. Oh, but it takes some nerve to be bold enough to grab things right out of people's yards." She made a face of displeasure.

Harry's expression matched his granddaughter's.

"I figure it's either someone no one would suspect or someone everyone would suspect, and we just need a little more time to fig-ure that part out," Patricia continued. "Debbie, may I have one of those lemon tarts too, please? Wrapped up to go? I'm going to enjoy it after my lunch later. I have two morning appointments and then a will to draft, and there's nothing like a good lemon tart to make dividing funds seem like fun. Wait." She held up a hand. "Make that two tarts, please. I think Mama's coming by at some point, and her eyes light up every time she sees a little bag from her favorite café."

"Two tarts it is." Debbie packaged the pastries and set them and Patricia's usual coffee order on the counter. "And give your mother my best."

"I will." Patricia slipped off the stool. She planted a kiss on Harry's weathered cheek before she gathered up her belongings. "Pop Pop, I love you."

"Love you too, sugar." He gave her a smile of such love that Debbie sighed to see it. Then he shifted his attention back to Debbie and his breakfast. "You know she might be onto something there with her idea about most likely and least likely."

Debbie wiped a cleaning cloth over the counter area Patricia had just vacated. "Most likely?"

"Kids with too much time on their hands."

"No disagreement there. What about least likely? Because that's who it often turns out to be, isn't it?"

Harry offered her a sage look. "I think it might be someone who wants the town to be noticed. Maybe someone who wants to solve their own mystery so they get credit. You see it on those crime shows all the time, how the criminal engineers the crime to be a hero."

Janet had just come through the swinging door separating the kitchen from the dining room and counter. She settled four boxes of assorted muffins onto the bakery display rack as she complimented Harry. "That's a solid idea, Harry. So we watch to see who's got something to gain."

"I'm not sure what kind of gain there is in used garden thingies, but I'm willing to keep an eye out."

"Me too," Janet said as a timer buzzed for her attention. She hurried back into the kitchen.

The café got busy and stayed that way throughout the day. The warmer weather, plus the looming threat of a three-day rain, tempted people out. Harry's rain prediction proved true. Julian's afternoon game was canceled, and he wasn't one bit happy about it. Debbie had just gotten to Greg's house when the late bus came by. It dropped the boys at the corner. They made a mad dash for the house as the driving rain soaked them, and when they got to the door, one of them—Debbie wasn't sure which—flung it open.

The door banged off the wall with a firm thud, came back, and smacked Julian into the rack of hooks on the mudroom wall. Greg must have emptied the hooks that weekend, so there were no cushy winter coats or ski pants to soften the blow. Julian's howl made that clear.

"Wouldn't have happened if you didn't always try to be first." Jaxon didn't soften the superiority in his tone. "I'm older. Faster. Stronger. Get used to it."

"You're also a jerk. I'm plenty used to that."

Debbie came their way, unsure what to do. They didn't fight often, but there was a tempest brewing now.

Julian's face was red. Tears filled his eyes. A mark on his cheek extended into his hairline, and he was rubbing his right arm.

She directed her attention to him. A little sympathy couldn't be a bad thing. "You okay, bud? How can I help?"

Her ploy fell flat. Julian scowled, and tears slipped down his cheeks. "Make the stupid rain stop, get me a new brother, and send this one to boarding school so he doesn't bother me anymore."

"Make it a southern one." Jaxon gave his brother a bored look. "Less rain. More games. I'd be down with that."

"More time for you to sit on the bench," Julian snapped, still rubbing his arm.

Jaxon's face went pale. He fisted his hands and stared at his younger brother. Then he turned abruptly and headed for the stairs. He didn't say a word, but it was clear that Julian's words hit their mark. He stomped up the stairs, muttering something under his breath.

Jaxon's skills at soccer secured a lot of playing time, but baseball was different. Where Julian started the games and often played straight through, Jaxon had been sharing time with two other sophomores on the JV squad. Debbie knew the score. To play varsity, you had to be the best at your position. Sitting the bench for half the game was a good indication that your coach didn't trust your skills. The varsity coach and the JV coach were brothers. They talked. If one thought Jaxon wasn't solid enough to be a starter, the other brother might agree.

That was a concern for another day. She reached out to Julian's shoulder. "Need ice?"

"No." He kept his gaze pointed toward the ground. His lower lip trembled. A tremble that Debbie felt come through the boy's shoulder, even with his light jacket on. "I just need it to stop raining. And I want my mom's statue back, but I don't think anyone cares about a stupid old gnome thing that has a chip on one shoe. Except me, I mean. Jaxon thinks I'm stupid for worrying about it."

Debbie's radar went on high alert. "He called you stupid?"

Julian shrugged one shoulder—the uninjured one—then sighed. "Not exactly. But he did say it's just an old statue. Nothing to get worked up about. Then he gave me that look."

She kept her hand on Julian's shoulder and prayed for the right words to say. "The police are looking. Janet and I are too. The mayor put a notice on social media to ask whoever's taken items to put them in the drop-off box over at the thrift store. Have you heard anything?" She moved back slightly to give him room to shed his wet hoodie, shoes, and the book bag. "Have the kids at school said anything about it?"

"No kid I know would want old garden stuff." He sounded glum. He looked the same way, and he kept his gaze averted while he peeled the wet jacket off. "I kept hoping that maybe Mrs. Haywood took her to fix her chipped foot. I showed it to her last year. She seemed sorry to see that Greta's foot was messed up, but if she took it, she'd have said something. Wouldn't she?"

"I can call her."

He shook his head. "Naw, that makes us sound weird, that we're hoping someone kidnapped our garden gnome to fix her foot when we didn't bother to do it ourselves."

Ouch. Debbie splayed her hands. "I would be happy to try to mend the plaster when we get her back. We can match the paint color too. I'm sorry I didn't realize she had a chip, Julian."

"Dad knew about it." His tone stayed grim. "Then he got busy doing things for other people, and nothing got fixed. Greta and Hans don't mean so much anymore."

"But they do." Debbie reached out and touched a finger to Julian's chin. The red mark from his bump into the hook was fading, but the tears weren't. He hadn't even bothered to wipe them away. "They will always mean something special, Julian. Your mom got them and loved them and loved you. They'll always have a special meaning here."

"Yeah, well, that didn't work out so good, did it?" He slung his book bag over his shoulder and trudged to the stairs. "I got my homework done because I thought we'd be at the baseball field."

"I'm sorry about the game."

Julian walked upstairs looking sad and withdrawn. Debbie had no idea how to help him.

CHAPTER SIX

Rain drilled the rooftop unceasingly, and when the impact seemed to soften, the lapse was short-lived. Between the drone of rain and the boys' stony silence, supper at the Connor house was not a happy meal. The boys retreated back to their rooms once the dishwasher was loaded and humming.

Greg let Hammer out for a last look outdoors. He winced when he closed the side door after the black-and-white border collie. "I used to think a long winter was bad for morale, but I think this rain is worse." He reached out and drew Debbie in while gusts of wind drove the rain against the back windows of the house.

She settled into the embrace and sighed softly. "Did you know Greta has a chip on one foot? A tip of her shoe is missing?" She leaned back against his arm and met his gaze.

He looked puzzled initially, then frowned. "I did. But I totally forgot until just now. Julian told me when we put them away last year. I said I'd patch it as soon as I could. Except I didn't. He brought that up?"

"This afternoon after his face and shoulder hit the coat hooks in the mud room."

"I can't believe I forgot all about that chip. He told me specifically, so why didn't I bring it in the house right then and fix it?"

"Busy working. Busy running kids around. Busy feeding kids." Debbie wouldn't fault him. He'd done an amazing job keeping things together as a single dad.

"Life's always busy with kids, but that's no excuse. I'm saying that because I *know* he's got a special bond with those two statues. To him, they're a link to the mother he barely remembers. We've got videos of him carrying them when he was just a little guy and helping Holly get them settled in the garden. It was a thing between the two of them. Jaxon would help too, but it wasn't a big deal to him. Julian was different. Almost protective of the statues. I should have fixed the stupid chip, and that's on me."

"Then we make that priority one when we find her." Debbie put her hands on his upper arms and squeezed lightly. "And we *will* find her."

He looked doubtful, but then Hammer pawed the back door to be let in. Greg kept a small stack of old, thirsty towels by the back door lately because Hammer's dense fur stayed wet a good long while without a nice rubdown. He opened the door for Hammer, expertly threw a towel over him, and began to rub before the dog could shake and send water droplets flying.

She bent and kissed Greg's cheek lightly. "There might be a silver lining to this weather. It might be obnoxious enough to keep our thief from nabbing anything else right now. I'll see you tomorrow." Greg began to rise, but she said, "Keep working on Hammer. I'll see myself out."

On her way to the front door, she paused by the stairs, wondering if she should go up and say goodbye. She voted that down as possibly intrusive. If the boys had their earbuds in, they wouldn't hear her call up the stairs, so that option was out. She settled for texting instead. HEADING OUT. SORRY ABOUT STUPID WEATHER. THANKS FOR YOUR HELP IN THE KITCHEN.

Jaxon texted back a thumbs-up emoji.

Julian didn't respond at first, but her phone signaled a text when she got into her car. She picked up the phone to check it before she backed out of the driveway. CAN YOU READ MY BOOK REPORT THIS WEEKEND?

Of course she would. She typed a quick reply. GLAD TO. LET ME KNOW WHEN.

She drove home, considering her earlier actions with the boys. Should she have scolded Jaxon? No. He hadn't deliberately body-checked his brother into the wall of coat hooks.

Scold them for racing into the house? That would be silly when it was pouring outside.

Expect more empathy from Jaxon or a little compassion? That made sense, but how did one instill that in a big brother who was spending time on the bench while little brother was the starting shortstop for the junior high team?

And she knew she had to tread lightly. She and Greg weren't married yet, she hadn't moved into their home, and the boys were almost certainly having complicated feelings about her. It wouldn't be normal if they weren't.

She broached the topic with Janet the next day. Janet's reply didn't offer a whole lot of help, but she confirmed the conclusion Debbie had come to after she got home. "This is all a big adjustment for them. Give them time," she advised as Paulette posted three new orders. It hadn't been busy. The gray skies and chronic drizzle dampened the mood of the entire town. "I know it sounds trite, but time really does heal a lot of wounds. Once the weather clears up and they're outside again, things will even out. I expect they're tired of being stuck inside. They got a taste of nice weather and loved it. This—" She aimed a look to the back windows where the rain drummed relentlessly. "This feels like solid regression."

Paulette made a wry face as she headed for the cooler. "Folks are grumpy today. Almost across the board. It doesn't look like the skies are going to clear up at all until Sunday afternoon." She gestured to the rear of the café. "Kim mentioned how that bedraggled tabby cat is cowering along the back wall again today. Do you mind if I put out a can of tuna for him?"

The cat had shown up the week before. Loose cats weren't unusual, but this one didn't seem to belong to anyone. Most indoor/outdoor cats would do their share of hunting along the railroad tracks, then head home for a nice snooze, but this guy seemed to take cover wherever he could. That meant he probably didn't have a place to call home.

"Absolutely," Debbie replied. "He's a pretty thing. But on the thin side, wouldn't you say?"

Greg's mother nodded. "Sure is. I could grab a bag of cat food at the market today. I know we shouldn't encourage strays, but we can't let him go hungry. I saw him come out from beneath the dumpster yesterday morning. I think that's where he's living."

Debbie exchanged a look with Janet as Paulette went back to the dining room. "You know, if we let Bernice know about this nice cat in need of a home—" She left the sentence open, waiting for Janet to fill in the missing piece.

"And she comes by to see him, we could carefully bring up the subject of yard decor?"

"Exactly."

"I'll give her a call. On speaker." Janet set the oven timer for her prebaked pie crusts and called Bernice. She explained their concerns, and Bernice was quick to reply.

"I will absolutely come by and see about this cat," she told them. "Maurice over at the gas station mentioned seeing a needy cat around too. That animal deserves a roof and good square meals. I'll come by tomorrow, rain or shine. Greg Connor and his dog are here today, and I don't dare leave. You never know when he might need a helping hand or just someone to hold the ladder. Those things get tippy, you know."

Debbie bit her tongue. Greg's ladders weren't the "tippy" sort. The self-leveling ladders were amazingly efficient devices and well worth the investment, but Bernice was old-school and then some. "I think that's wonderful," Janet assured the elderly woman. "We'll see you tomorrow."

Bernice wasn't quite done yet. "Does he let you get near?"

"Not even close," admitted Janet. "He shies back."

"Well, most people don't do it right, that's a simple fact. Although I know people seem intent to try, even when they should stand back and give me a call. That's the way of things, I suppose." The resignation in her tone underscored her meaning.

"You've got a knack," Janet replied. "And we'll look forward to seeing you tomorrow."

"I'll be there on the early side," Bernice promised. "That way I've got all day if need be."

"We'll have coffee waiting."

"I'll take tea. I'm a little off coffee at the moment."

"Of course." Janet exchanged a quick smile with Debbie as she disconnected the call. "You know there's no denying her knack with cats."

"Her unpredictable treatment of humans gets her some funny looks," noted Debbie. "But she told me that she's rehomed over thirty-five cats since I've been back. Thirty-five cats in two years is significant."

"It sure is. But I'm hoping the garage full of yard stuff isn't an indicator that she's in some kind of mental decline." Janet removed the large mixing bowl from her mixer as she spoke. "Bernice is quirky, but she's got a big heart and treasures her independence. I don't want to see her lose it."

Debbie didn't want to see that either, but a text from Greg less than an hour later seemed to raise more questions about the elderly woman's collection. No GRETA, he wrote. I DON'T SEE PATRICIA'S SIGN EITHER. OR ANY OF THE OTHER MISSING ITEMS. BUT THERE ARE MORE THINGS IN THE GARAGE NOW. IT'S BEEN POURING FOR THE LAST THIRTY-SIX HOURS. WHERE DID THEY COME FROM?

Debbie decided a phone call was better than a text. She hit Greg's number, and he answered quickly. "Hey. What's up?"

The tenderness in his voice made her smile. "I can take a quick break right now, so I thought I'd call. Can you ask her?" she wondered. "Ask Bernice what she's doing with all the yard decor? Casually?"

"I tried that," Greg admitted. "It seemed like the easiest path to take. She gave me a scolding look and made sure the garage door was shut firmly. Then she crossed her arms and tapped her toe."

Debbie had seen that stance before. When Bernice did that, it did not bode well for the other person or persons. "Oh, wow."

"Yep. She nailed me with eyebrows drawn and said it's best if I focus on my work because that's what I was there for. I took the hint and didn't press further. Since I'm working at the other end of the house, it doesn't make sense for me to get into the garage anymore. Not at the moment, anyway."

"I guess you've done what you can do." Debbie shrugged on her end. "But thank you for looking. For Greta, I mean. I know you're not a snoop. Does she mind Hammer being there?" The dog liked to tag along with Greg. He was happy going house to house and didn't mind sitting in the cab of the truck, watching for Greg's return. His dedication was a wonderful thing to see.

"Not at all. In fact, she said he could have the run of her fenced back yard if that would suit him, but on a day like today he's happier in the truck."

"I can't blame him there. Oops, orders coming in. I'll see you tonight."

"You sure will."

The rain continued as predicted. Light showers stayed steady throughout Saturday and into Sunday and then, like someone flipped a switch, the weather broke on Sunday afternoon. The sun came out and flooded the area with bright golden light. It was an instant mood-changer.

People came out of their houses. They walked for ice cream. They snapped pictures of the high water along the creek and the flooded conditions of part of the town's baseball fields. Birds began singing again, bright songs with cheerful tones. By the time Debbie and Janet headed for the bridal shop in New Philadelphia late Monday afternoon, Dennison seemed bathed in the bright colors of spring.

Janet insisted on driving. "It's my turn to spoil you and your mom," she told Debbie and Mom. "I've waited a long time to escort the bride and the mother-of-the-bride on this jaunt." She jangled her keys and indicated Mom's SUV. "Let's go see about a dress!"

"I gassed it up, so we won't have to stop at all." Janet's mother settled into the middle of the roomy back seat. Debbie's mom slid in on one side, and Paulette did the same on the other.

They made it to the five o'clock appointment a few minutes early. That gave them time to peruse the bridal side of the store while they waited for their consultant. Three other brides were being helped.

Not one of them was over thirty. Well, one might be but not by much. Debbie suddenly felt old, even though she knew that was ridiculous. Brides came in all shapes, sizes, and ages.

Debbie looked toward the sea of white stretching out before her. Three mannequins sported gorgeous gowns. One displayed a fitted mermaid contour, the next a simple, elegant chiffon dress, and the last a ballerina-style princess gown.

As the dressing rooms opened and young women stepped out to show friends and family the sample gowns they'd chosen to try on, Debbie was pretty sure she was in the wrong place at the wrong time, because she couldn't see herself wearing any one of these dresses.

Ever.

She took a deep breath.

Just as she was about to grab Janet's arm and make a beeline for the car, a woman approached them. She smiled as if in recognition. "Debbie Albright?"

Caught! She nodded. "Yes. And this is my best friend and matron of honor, Janet Shaw."

"Of course it is." The consultant scored serious points with Debbie when she motioned to a quiet corner, away from the gowns and the people. "Can we sit? Talk?"

Debbie grabbed the invitation like a lifeline. "Yes. Please."

"I'm Kathy Penwallader," the woman told them as Janet and Debbie took seats at a sturdy white table. Paulette, Mom, and Lorilee followed them over. Twinkle lights added warm sparkle to the cozy area and the ceiling above. "I retired from my position at a local plumbing company about ten years ago now, but I'm not the sort to sit home. When my sister offered me this job, I jumped at it. Working with brides and their families, helping them coordinate things according to their vision, makes me happy. And my husband likes it when I'm happy. He probably also likes it that I'm out of the house now and again." She laughed at this last part, and everyone laughed with her.

"Retirement can be too much of a good thing. I'm Lorilee Hill. Janet's mom."

"And I'm Becca Albright."

"And I'm Paulette." She extended her hand in greeting. "Mother of the groom."

Debbie took a deep breath. With the easy conversation, she was feeling a bit less awkward about being here. "So, Mrs. Penwallader—"

"Kathy will do quite nicely." The bridal consultant smiled. "I'm here to listen," she assured them. "Brides are as unique as the stars above, and I have never believed that my job is to sell you something. Rather, it's to see if we can find a good match. When we do that, everything else falls into place. That makes the process so much easier, takes the anxiety over finding the one right dress out of the equation."

Kathy's words landed like balm for Debbie's soul. "I was nearly ready to race for the door," she admitted, and Kathy laughed.

"I know a deer-in-the-headlights look when I see one," she said. "It's natural, because there's so much put on the notion of finding the one-and-only perfect dress these days. Saying yes to *the dress.*" She stressed the last two words. "And having it perfect. Yet for hundreds, even thousands of years, women got married in the best dress they already owned with not much thought to anything else, because there was work to do and food to find. There were homes to tend, prairies to tame, houses to build. It's only in recent times that we've exaggerated the importance of the gown when what we should be examining is the importance of the marriage itself."

"First and foremost," Debbie's mother agreed.

"So let's just have fun," Kathy suggested. "Share any ideas you might have with me now, and I'd also ask you to be open to suggestions, even if the dress doesn't look its best on the hanger. A dress can be transformed when put on the right person."

It made sense to Debbie. "That sounds good. It sounds wonderful, in fact. A-line is my go-to style, and I tend toward sleeves. Also..." She hesitated slightly before finishing this thought. "I've never been the sort to enjoy being the center of attention."

"Good to know." Kathy stood and indicated the quieter side of the gown display area. "Janet, will you be my assistant? Help me dress the bride?"

"I'd be delighted!"

Forty-five minutes later, Janet put her hands on her hips after adjusting the latest gown. Debbie saw her pursed lips in the mirror. "You hate it."

Janet immediately looked guilty and righted her expression. "Do *you* love it? That's the important thing."

"It's lovely, but no. Still, it would do if we don't find one that screams *buy me!* in large-font letters."

Kathy had stepped out of the room to gather a few more dresses.

Janet opened the door of the large dressing room, and Debbie turned to face the trio of mothers.

Debbie's mother was the first to speak. "It's beautiful, darling. What do you think?"

Debbie smoothed a hand over the thin chiffon outer layer. "It's lovely."

"Gorgeous," agreed Lorilee.

"But you're not shining," noted Paulette. "So perhaps a backup alternative?"

Debbie shared an understanding expression with Greg's mother. "My thoughts exactly."

"You know, it's hard when every dress we try looks good." Kathy came up alongside with two more gowns and spoke matter-of-factly. "You've got a beautiful figure, you're tall enough to carry just about any style, and you move gracefully."

"Well, thank you." Debbie turned back to the trifold full-length mirror and touched the gown gently. "It is quite pretty."

"And yet..." Kathy moved forward and hung the new selections on the heavy-duty hook inside the dressing room. "Not quite there."

"But it could be a possibility," Debbie told her. In truth, all the gowns she'd tried on were beautiful, but none of them stood out the way she'd thought a wedding gown was supposed to.

"Now I'd like you to humor me." Kathy indicated the new gowns hanging on the side wall. "We've got some different looks here. Unique. Nothing like the styles we've tried on so far."

"Which has been a long list of A-line and empire-waisted varieties with no puff," Janet observed.

Debbie met Janet's eyes in the mirror. "You know I'm not a puff kind of person." Debbie was fairly certain nothing could change her mind about that.

The second gown of the new choices proved her wrong.

She took one look in the mirror and fell silent. Tears pricked her eyes.

"Oh my." Janet pressed her hands together, and the moment she saw Debbie's eyes get watery, hers did the same.

"Stop that," Debbie whispered.

Janet waved her off, half laughing, half crying. "No one cries alone in my presence. You of all people should know that. So what do you think? Are you as over-the-moon about this dress as I am?"

"Yes. Absolutely. It's nothing like I envisioned a forty-something Debbie wearing, but it is absolutely perfect." She'd have scoffed at the idea of a traditional style wedding gown, but the full skirt on this satin-and-lace dress moved with her. The fitted waist showed off her figure and the sweetheart bodice left the perfect neckline for her grandmother's sapphire necklace—her something old and something blue. Her grandmother had given it to Debbie before she passed away. She'd said, "Something from me for your wedding day."

For twenty years Debbie hadn't thought this day would ever happen. Seeing her reflection in the mirror, in this dress, reaffirmed the current reality. She was soon to be a bride.

And she'd found the perfect dress.

"Should I open the door? Let the mothers see?"

"Yes. Let's." Debbie turned on the platform.

Kathy opened the door, and all three mothers reacted with sighs and flurries of positive words. They loved the gown, yes, but Debbie was pretty sure that what they loved most was her reaction to the dress. When they were done dabbing their eyes and smiling, Kathy faced Debbie squarely. "So. Are we good?"

Debbie didn't have to be asked twice. "Couldn't be better."

"And in less than ninety minutes with time for a nice dinner!" Her mother laughed as she hugged Debbie one more time. She got teary-eyed, then laughed again. When Kathy offered a generous discount for buying the store sample instead of ordering a new gown from the manufacturer, Debbie was even happier. "I'll set you up for your initial fitting with Clara, our seamstress," Kathy told her. "She's just caught up with prom dresses, so I can fit you in this Thursday afternoon at four thirty. Does that work for you?"

Bridal magazines had advised that it could take weeks or months to get her dress properly fitted, so the thought of a Thursday appointment seemed marvelous. "It does. Thank you."

"And I insist on paying for this dress." Mom made the announcement as Kathy finished filling out the paperwork. "I know we're sharing expenses for the wedding, but it's a mother's right to buy her daughter's wedding gown. I'm exercising that privilege right now."

Debbie gave her a big hug. "I will accept that kindness gratefully. Isn't it beautiful, Mom?"

Her mother smiled into Debbie's eyes and had to blink back tears—just a few—as she agreed. "Yes. Yes, it is. I knew it the moment I saw that look on your face."

"Greg will love it." Paulette opened the shop door for the other women as they filed out. "Not only is his bride stunningly beautiful, she makes great homemade pizza. What's not to love?"

Her comment made Debbie laugh, just as an incoming text sounded. She settled into the passenger seat and opened the text. "Greta!"

"They found her?" Janet turned quickly. She'd put the key in the ignition, but didn't turn the car on. "Where?"

"Not found." Debbie held her phone up so the moms in the back could see the text from Greg. "She's on social media. Even shared on the town's website. Someone who's using the name 'NoPlaceLikeGnome' posted comments with Greta's pictures in front of different businesses."

Who would do this? Steal something small and inconsequential to others, then post about it on social media? As if it was okay to mock their loss?

"Do you think Tucker Lewis could be responsible for something like this?" Janet met Debbie's eye. "You know how much he loved that Texas scary doll thing. He thought it was crazy clever and talked about it for weeks. How those funny videos brought life to the town. He's been saying how he wanted to boost the engagement on the town's social media sites. Something like this would be right up his alley."

Debbie recalled Ian coming into the café a few months ago and telling them about Tucker's reaction. She'd looked it up later online and remembered now that a small police department in Texas had discovered a creepy-looking Victorian doll on a town bench outside the police station. CCTV footage had shown several giggling teenage girls dropping the doll off at the bench before driving away.

Seizing the opportunity, the town's officers did parody videos of the doll sneaking up on them. The videos went viral, and Tucker had thought it was a perfect, opportunistic way to increase traffic on the Texas town's pages.

"Tucker would never actually steal things, though, would he?" Debbie shook her head. "I can't see him doing that. Except he did mention that fewer people were clicking on the posts, and he does like that back-and-forth between shop owners, residents, and the town. But why would he take things? It's Tucker. Why wouldn't he just ask to borrow them?"

Janet splayed her hands. "I don't know, but I think we need to talk with him."

"Tonight?" Mom and Lorilee spoke at once.

Debbie shook her head. She wanted to know more. She wanted to know who'd produced these funny images of little Greta gallivanting around their town. But she wasn't likely to find out anything more tonight, and the group was excited about a lovely dinner together.

Debbie turned and offered the trio of mothers a warm smile. "Not tonight. Tonight we celebrate finding the dress, setting up the fitting, and having dinner. The posts make it clear that Greta is fine.

Someone appears to be taking good care of her. Although the whole thing is bold, isn't it? To take her, then post about her."

Janet agreed. "It is, and we're going to figure out just who's got that kind of nerve. We might be able to trace back to the poster to figure out who this is. I texted Ian to see if that's possible."

A few minutes later, Ian called them as Janet pulled into a parking space alongside the restaurant. His voice rang through the speaker system.

"I've done a trace back on the poster. It's a new account with no followers or friends. Someone's gone incognito."

"So they're clever with the internet," Janet offered. "Or at least just set up the profile very recently, and there hasn't been time for anyone to follow or friend them."

"Seems so," Ian said. "We'll have tech go deeper. On the bright side, Greta's trek about town has already gotten over fifty positive reactions."

"Greta's going viral," Debbie said.

"Could be. Viral by our standards, anyway. Her pictures are gaining traction on other sites too. Sorry, Debbie." He sounded truly contrite. "It's not cool that someone is flaunting your loss like this."

Debbie hesitated a moment before replying. Then she said, "She looks kind of cute, Ian."

Ian started to say something, but Debbie went on. "I'm mad that someone took her and about the worry it's caused the boys, but whoever is doing this has gotten really creative. She's wearing different clothes in a couple of the shots. And carrying tiny shopping bags, advertising the shops on Grant Street. I only wish they'd asked, first."

"Agreed," Ian said. "You ladies have a nice dinner. We'll see what we can track down."

Just knowing that another very important item was checked off the list helped make it a joyous occasion. It opened the conversation about the wedding, and she didn't find the conversation as stressful as she normally did. Was that because she'd completed a crucial component? Or because she was surrounded by people who loved her?

Probably a combination of both, she realized as the evening wound down.

Greg was waiting for her at her home when Janet dropped her off ninety minutes later. He spent a few moments greeting the other women, but once they'd gone, he faced Debbie on her classic craftsman-style front porch.

She reached out and took his hands in hers. "Did the boys see Greta's pictures?" she asked. "How did they handle it? Are they upset?"

"They're not happy about it. They feel like someone's mocking them, and I can't disagree."

Debbie unlocked the front door, and Greg followed her inside. When she faced him again, she read a sadness in his eyes. A look that hadn't been noticeable on the porch. She took his hands again and planted a kiss on his cheek. "What is it? What's wrong?"

"Her foot."

It took Debbie a moment to realize the import of what Greg was saying. "Greta's?"

He nodded. Then he sighed before pulling her into his arms for a hug. "It's fixed."

She drew back, surprised. "The chip on her foot?"

"It's fixed. Plus her shoes look fresh and new, like she's had a touch-up."

"Or a full-on makeover." Debbie held his gaze. "New clothes, shopping bags, and mended shoes. Who on earth is doing this and why?"

And for the first time since she'd met him, Greg seemed totally mystified and even a little lost. "I don't know," he said. "But it was the first thing that Julian noticed. He said, 'At least someone fixed her foot.' It just about broke my heart."

CHAPTER SEVEN

arry came strolling into the café the next morning, whistling an old Glenn Miller tune. He greeted Debbie with a broad smile, and Crosby, bless his heart, seemed to be smiling too.

"Harry, you're later than normal today, and hearing that music's got me in mind to do a little swing dancing around this dining room before we get busy." Debbie met his smile with one of her own as she restocked clean silverware in the tray beneath the counter. "You look positively jaunty."

"I'm in that good a mood," he told her as he slipped onto his favorite stool. "Patricia called me less than half an hour ago with some good news! You know the sign that disappeared?"

"The one you gave Sylvia," said Debbie.

"That's the one," he declared as Crosby settled on the floor alongside him. "It's back." His smile brightened the room. "She went outside to get her paper from the box, and there it was, right where it had been before it went missing. Now isn't that a nice bit of news when someone repents of this or that and decides to do the right thing?"

"It is." Debbie didn't try to mask her surprise as she set a napkin and silverware on the counter for Harry's breakfast. "I wonder how Patricia felt when she spotted it."

Patricia happened to walk in the door right then, and the smartly dressed attorney answered Debbie's question herself. "I was delighted," she told them warmly. "But add surprised and taken aback to that list. I don't like the idea of someone creeping around my yard taking things out and putting them back with me not hearing, seeing, or knowing a thing about it. That's not exactly a comfort for a woman living alone."

"Disconcerting to say the least," offered Debbie, and Patricia agreed as she slid onto the stool alongside her grandfather.

"While I'm glad to have Nana's sign back, I can't say I'm a fan of the shenanigans going on in our little town." She placed her stylish laptop bag on the empty stool on her right. "But I know just where to come and get something wonderful and a little decadent to soothe my rumpled emotions." She winked at Debbie and pointed a manicured finger toward the bakery case. "I've a mind to have one of those spring-themed cupcakes for my lunch dessert today. And my signature coffee, of course. Extra hot."

"Coming right up," Debbie told her, then directed her attention back to Harry. "What sounds good this morning, my friend?"

"Two eggs and toast, and we'll slip one of them to my walking partner here, if you don't mind. I'm eating light today."

"For any particular reason, my friend?" Debbie asked.

"I've got a full-on meal later, and it's better to save some room."

"A ploy I often use myself," Debbie told him.

"I'm on it!" Janet called out from the kitchen. "I'm just going to tuck these little delights into the case, and I'll head back to the kitchen and crack some eggs." She came through the swinging door with a tray of Jan Hagel cookies. "All this talk of gnomes had me thinking of these beauties. I haven't made them in a while." She settled the buttery almond Dutch shortbreads into the far side of the bakery case then hurried back to the kitchen while Debbie began making Patricia's peppermint mocha.

"This smells so good, I'm tempted to make one for myself," she confessed as she swirled a generous topping of whipped cream across the hot surface. She followed with a ribbon of peppermint syrup before she slipped the plastic cap over the layered drink. As she handed the delicious confection to Patricia, the café door opened and Bernice Byrne came in.

Bernice never took great pains with her appearance. Today's outfit consisted of worn jeans, a T-shirt that read "Cat Woman," and an old denim vest that looked like it was from the '70s. "I've got a few things to say," she announced as she stepped up to the counter on the other side of Harry, just to the right of Crosby. "The first being I gave a look out for that cat you called me about and didn't see hide nor hair of him."

"He's a now-you-see-him, now-you-don't kind of visitor," said Janet as she brought a second tray of cookies through. Snickerdoodles, this time. "But thank you so much for coming around to check on him. He's down a few meals, from the look of him, and no one has a knack for catching stray cats like you, Bernice."

Bernice offered her a sage nod. "Cat genes. My mama had 'em too. Enough sense to half know what they're thinking and figure out what's gonna tempt them into a comfy cage if needed. Though I'd be too humble by half to pretend I even *need* a cage most of the time. Patience, a little food, just the right number of words, and a steady hand works best."

Debbie had seen lots of people try to mimic Bernice's gift. It hadn't worked for any of them over the last two years, so she gave praise where praise was due. "You're amazing with them, Bernice. I think of all the cats you've rehomed, and it makes me smile. How's everything going up at your place?"

"That man of yours is a wonderful fixer." She slipped onto the stool and folded her hands. "He did some plumbing, then took care of some electrical things that weren't doing what they were made to do, all before he took down a half wall that was nothing but a bother. He got it all fixed back up and painted. It's like a whole new place, nice and open like people do now. Freshened things right up. I was thinking about taking a walk around town, keeping an eye out for the cat," she went on. "I'm heading up Third Street right off, so if you see him, give me a holler, will you? I've got my phone right here." She withdrew a flip phone that looked too old to still be in service.

"I've got your number from the last time you helped on a cat rescue here," Debbie assured the elderly woman. "I'll give you a call right away. Would you like something to go? A tea or a breakfast sandwich?"

Bernice slid off the stool and shook her head. "Eyes sharp and hands free." She patted the pocket of her seventies-style denim vest. "Treats here, and there." She indicated the second pocket of the vest with a quick nod. "Come prepared or don't bother showing up."

"That's the kind of motto that gets things done," noted Harry, and Bernice acknowledged his praise with a tip of her index finger to her forehead.

"I concur. I'll see you all later."

She strode out, resolute as she headed through the outer door and up the street.

Patricia accepted her cupcake bag from Debbie at the cash register. "That was a good reminder that we still have some good people in this town." She tapped her card against the icon as Debbie finished the transaction. "Even if we do have some oddballs taking stuff and then bringing them back when people aren't looking. You all have a nice day now."

"You too."

Before she left she leaned over and kissed her grandfather's cheek. "See you later, Pop Pop. Love you!"

"I love you too." Harry beamed as she went out the door, then redirected his attention to Debbie. "That girl makes us proud every single day and not just because she's a big-shot lawyer, you know."

Debbie hid a smile. "More because she's just plain nice inside and out, and everyone knows that about her. Should we give Crosby his egg outside or in, today?"

"He does love the sun," said Debbie, and Harry quickly agreed. She set the over-easy egg on the back step. When Crosby had finished cleaning every smidge from the disposable plate, he licked his chops. Then he wandered over to the big tree, did his customary three-circle spin, and lay down as if in desperate need of a nap.

"That's a dog's life," noted Harry. He jutted his chin toward the animal that had become his constant companion years before. "If I sat around as much as Crosby, my doc would be reading me the riot act and telling me exercise keeps the joints moving."

"You're not wrong." Debbie dropped the disposable plate into the wastebasket before washing her hands. "But Crosby's not a bit overweight, so you must be doing something right, my friend. Oh, Harry. See what we've got on the left over there?" She pointed out the back window, the one facing the train tracks. "There's the cat. The one Bernice came into town to find."

Bent low, the cat crept along the edge of the track fencing. He walked with a lion's gait, paw after determined paw, but in such a stealthy fashion that if you didn't know to look for the cat, you might not notice it.

Janet brought out another tray of cookies. She slid it into the opposite end of the case and followed the direction of Debbie's gaze. "Well, look who's come to pay us a visit."

Debbie pulled her phone out and called Bernice. "He's here," she whispered into the phone, as if speaking normally might startle the cat.

It wouldn't, of course. The cat was outside and on the far side of the wrought iron fence. The orange tabby couldn't possibly hear her, so she raised her voice back to normal. "He's creeping along the fence by the tracks."

The moment she spoke at a normal volume, the cat bolted.

Debbie stared at the phone, then the fence, then Janet and Harry. "That cat couldn't have heard me. Not way over there. Right?"

"Pure coincidence," said Harry, but he said it with a twinkle in his eye. "Though I've been told that cat hearing is uncommonly sensitive."

"No." Debbie frowned before readdressing Bernice. "He took off, Bernice. Heading west, up the tracks. I'm so sorry."

"Not one thing to worry about," Bernice replied. "I'm marking the day and time for every instance we see him come about. Cats are creatures of habit most of the time. Like us, eh? So I'll make a note of every time we see him. That helps set the strategy. Keep your eyes peeled. Okay?"

"Yes, ma'am."

Debbie ended the call. The café started to get busy then, typical for a weekday opening. By the time things slowed at half past one, they'd had a banner day.

"Who'd have thought we'd be this busy on a random Tuesday in April?"

Debbie didn't pose the question to anyone in particular, but Paulette indicated the sunny day outdoors with a flick of her dish-cloth as she wiped tables. "Nice weather, bright sun, gentle breeze. The birds are back too. I have two male robins that keep going chest to chest in the backyard."

"Which one will win the fair maid's heart?" wondered Janet, and Paulette laughed.

"The one that's helping her build the nest," she replied. "I'm not even sure it's one of the fighting pair, but there's one male that's on hand all the time, bringing bits of dried grass, twigs, and weeds. He's a keeper."

Janet's phone buzzed. She opened it, frowned, then said, "Ian says, 'Trying to trace the social media poster back hasn't turned up anything. We also checked to see if anyone's doorbell cameras captured someone taking these pics, but nothing of note. Yet.'"

Debbie sighed. "It's bad enough that whoever is doing this is holding our little gnome hostage, but he or she made Greg feel absolutely awful when he saw the pictures, because whoever took Greta fixed her foot."

"What?" Paulette and Janet spoke in unison. Paulette pressed further. "What does that mean, Debbie?"

"Greta's foot had a chip in the plaster," she explained. "A significant one. It happened last year sometime. Julian had asked Greg to fix it last fall, and Greg said he would. Then the gnomes got put away, and when Julian brought the gnomes out last week, Greta's foot still had a piece missing. Anyway, if you look at the online images, her foot's been fixed. That made Greg feel awful. A complete stranger thought enough of the gnome to fix the foot, and he didn't."

Compassion softened Paulette's features. "Julian takes things to heart, then wears his heart on his sleeve. He hardly ever asks for anything, so I can see how that would hit Greg like an arrow to the chest."

"Exactly."

A few last-minute customers stopped in for coffee. Janet took care of them while Debbie finished the kitchen duties. They were just about to lock up for the day when a Mennonite woman came through the door.

She glanced around and then sighed as if… well, Debbie wasn't sure why she sighed, but as Debbie and Janet moved her way, she lifted her gaze to Janet. "Open, *ja*?"

"Barely!" Janet offered the woman a broad smile. "The kitchen's closed, but the baked goods are all available. How are you, Rhonda? It's so good to see you!"

"For me as well." That was what the woman said, but it didn't sound quite as sincere as it should. Her voice was hesitant, a certain reluctance coloring her tone.

"Debbie." Janet turned to make introductions. "This is Rhonda Bontrager from Sugarcreek. Her family runs the lumberyard and a sizable furniture-making business up there."

Debbie recognized the name right off. "My mom's porch swing came from your place." She reached out to shake the woman's hand. "It's beautiful. I love the intricate hearts in the back. We call it the Sweetheart Swing."

"Swings and benches are two of my husband's specialties," the woman replied. Her voice sounded brighter than it had moments before. "He takes joy in doing a good job. Well." She sighed, this time for real. "He did."

Janet moved forward, looking concerned. "Rhonda, what's happened?"

"Ephraim needed to get his knee fixed," Rhonda said. "So we set up his appointment with the surgeons in New Philadelphia. They did the surgery a few weeks ago. All seemed well until the end of March. Now something has gone wrong. The knee is infected. He cannot work, he is on medications, and I expect you know what it is like when a man cannot get his work done."

Janet nodded. "Ian got cellulitis a few years back, and he was a bear. It took way too long to clear up, and he wasn't happy about it. Do you need help, Rhonda? Is there something we can do?"

"No, my *Englisch* nephew has come." She gestured toward the street side of the café. The small depot parking lot separated the historic building from the vintage gazebo between the café and Grant Street. "Benjamin has been an immense help. He is my brother's eldest. He was born with a great imagination, so he is a good one for keeping Ephraim's mind off things. I do not know what I would do without him right now." She hesitated, then said, "We needed to come down this way for a physical therapy appointment, and I wanted to stop by and get a few things from your bakery case. I have not been here since you opened, and your families have always supported our businesses."

"Happily," Debbie assured her.

"It was time for me to do the same." Rhonda offered them a sincere smile. "You know how I loved the things you made on Third Street, Janet."

Janet moved to the case where they stored the leftover bakery goods at the end of the day. "I remember my old job fondly. What can we pack up for you?"

The Mennonite woman followed Janet, and it didn't take her long to make her decisions. "A dozen of those Jan Hagel cookies and four of those cupcakes, please."

Janet packaged the baked goods quickly. Rhonda paid with cash, and Janet handed her a receipt, smiling. "Please give Ephraim our best. I'm sorry he's laid up. If it's all right, I'd like to add him to the prayer list at church."

"Prayers are welcome, and so are your good wishes. I will be off." She clutched the two small bags in her hand and headed for the door. When she got outside she paused momentarily at the street, looked both ways, then hurried on to a gray car parked in the depot lot. A younger man wearing jeans, sneakers, and a plaid flannel shirt hopped out of the driver's seat. He circled the car and opened Rhonda's door for her. Then he waited until she had her long skirt safely tucked inside before gently shutting the door. Only then did he get behind the wheel and drive away.

"What would we do without family?" Janet asked.

"My parents were a huge help to my grandmother and her sister when they got ill years ago. And look how Kim has taken such good care of Eileen all this time," Debbie said. "It's wonderful that the Bontragers have someone like that to help out."

Kim was giving the ticket office and the old depot waiting room a spring cleaning. She waved goodbye to Janet and Debbie as they came through a few moments later. As they crossed the street to the municipal parking lot, Ian came their way. He drew close and held up his phone. "Our culprit strikes again."

Once again, the Connors' gnome was being shared on social media.

Greta standing outside an ice cream shop with a sign that read OPEN FOR THE SEASON!

Greta, on a park swing, smiling at the camera.

Greta, feeding the ducks that liked to congregate at the village pond. The caption—LIVING HER BEST LIFE—hit Debbie hard. "What does that mean, exactly?" she fumed. "'Living her best life?' Nonsense. Her best life is being where she's supposed to be, in the Connor garden. It's not for someone else to decide what a gnome's best life is. Right?"

Janet and Ian exchanged looks, and then Ian said, "Since gnomes aren't actually alive..."

Debbie dropped her chin and sighed. "I know. It's just that whoever is doing this is pushing my buttons. Strangely more so now that he or she doesn't seem to be doing any harm and it's all a joke. Except that every time they post a picture of her, it pours salt in the wound."

"And how are they getting pictures of her here, there, and everywhere without anyone seeing the photographer or the setup?" Janet asked.

"The shots could have been taken anytime," Ian told them. "Our IT guy said that the poster is inserting Greta and the words into the scenes using technology. If you look, you can tell he or she is altering the scenes slightly too. The colors are richer and more vibrant than they are in person. We actually checked a couple of the shots from the photo's vantage point, and a toybox had been cropped out of one and a pair of bikes, lying on the ground, out of another."

"The colors pop." Debbie examined the posts more closely. "Do you think they used a filter to brighten things up?"

Ian shrugged. "Possibly. Certainly not my area of expertise. But they're definitely enhanced. And check out the flowers in the new urns."

Debbie let out a whoosh of breath. "Those new urns aren't getting planted for a few more weeks, as far as I know."

"Exactly." Ian squared his shoulders. "So whoever is doing this wants the town to look its best. Even before everything is in place for the season. As if he or she wants to showcase the town like it could be. The photos make everything wonderful, and you know that the end of winter in a northern town isn't exactly what any of us would call pretty."

"Other than the mayor, there's only one person in town who'd want to promote the village this way, and we all know who that is." Debbie handed the phone back to Ian, folded her arms, and tapped her toe. "Tucker's been sharing the posts. And he did take those community education photography courses a year or so ago. He talked about it online."

Ian appeared less certain. "Tucker does like the village to get its share of notice." He paused. He'd never been the kind of guy to jump on bandwagons or speak carelessly about people or events. It was another quality that made him a great lawman and town leader. "He's a great promoter, but I can't picture him taking things out of people's yards. I'll check with him, but he's at a municipal conference in Cincinnati. He won't be back until after the weekend."

Debbie didn't know Tucker Lewis well, but she was aware of his feelings about their hometown. He was justifiably proud of the upgraded image they'd worked hard to achieve. In less than six years the town had demolished multiple eyesore buildings, received funds to upgrade other buildings and streets, encouraged new growth, and had received well-deserved grants and donations to renovate both the historic depot area and the town's vintage business district. "I'm not thrilled with anyone messing with a pair of perfectly wonderful boys who just want their mother's gnome back. Can't we ask Tucker about it while he's away? Call him?"

Ian splayed his hands. "We could, but we don't have any real indication that it is Tucker, Debbie. Other than his love for this town and his devotion to giving it a great social media presence. Plus this conference shouldn't be leaving him a lot of time to mess with pictures, although maybe if you're that good, it doesn't take all that long." He shrugged. "Again, not my area of expertise. Let's wait until he's back, okay? I'd feel better about approaching it then. It gives me time to examine other possibilities."

Debbie knew he was right, but she didn't have to like it. Then she glanced down at the inviting gnome pictures on Ian's phone again. "It's not that I mind the idea behind this funny little statue having the time of her life. If she wasn't stolen property, I'd think it was darling."

"Which is exactly how over two hundred people have reacted so far," Ian told her. "Our village's pages have never attracted attention like this. We get twenty or thirty reactions on a really good day, but people are in love with this whole thing. Although I don't think Greg's going to be amused when he sees it."

When Greg called Debbie about forty-five minutes later, it didn't take long to know that Ian had been right. She'd made a quick trip to the grocery store on her way home and got his call as she pulled into her driveway. "Hey, you. I'm meeting you at Jaxon's game in twenty minutes, right?"

"Yes. Bring a warm coat. I just swung by the house to grab one for myself. The temperature's dropping. Did you see the new pictures of Greta?"

His voice sounded hard and unyielding. Pretty atypical for the hardworking, compassionate man she'd fallen in love with over the last two years. "Yes. Ian showed me."

"I don't get it. Any of it," Greg went on. "First, taking something that doesn't belong to you, then flaunting what you've done by posting pics of it all over town on the internet. What kind of person—"

He stopped, and silence filled the air space. Then he said, "She's back."

"What?" By now Debbie was lugging in two sacks of groceries, and her phone was squeezed between her cheek and her shoulder.

She wrangled her way into the kitchen and maneuvered the two bags onto the table. "Who's back? Where exactly are you?"

"I'm home. In my driveway. And there, right where she's supposed to be, is Greta."

"Really?" That was music to Debbie's ears. "Greg, that's wonderful! The boys will be so excited to have her back."

"Well…"

"Well what?"

He sighed. "They would be. Except now—Hans is gone."

CHAPTER EIGHT

It took Debbie a moment for his words to sink in. "You're kidding. Right?"

"I'm not, and I'm going to check the Tinsdales' doorbell camera to see if it's caught anything today. I mean, it's broad daylight. Who has the gall to go into someone's yard and take things in broad daylight?"

Debbie posed a question that he might not have considered. "Did you park in the turnaround last night like you usually do?"

"Yes." He paused as he processed her question. "I get what you're saying. I was in the turnaround, then I drove out for work this morning. I probably wouldn't have noticed if Greta was there and Hans was gone, because the truck was pointed forward."

"Exactly. Which means someone could have done it last night. You had no reason to look back at the gardens."

"No line of sight from that vantage point. You're right," he admitted. He sighed. "It could have happened overnight, and it wouldn't have registered because I was focused ahead. The boys wouldn't have noticed either. It's still pretty dark when they get on the bus, and they're usually groggy in the morning. Normal teenagers."

"That's probably accurate," she agreed. "So the good thing is that Greta's back. My guess is we'll be seeing her buddy show up on social media soon. Someone is having a bit of a lark."

Greg didn't sound at all amused. "Stolen property isn't a lark."

"It's not," she agreed. "And I'm sorry that someone is messing with this. Someone with a fairly clever imagination. Greg..." She paused as a new idea occurred to her. "What about Julian's friend? Kelsey Addison? Remember how Julian said she was great with technology? That she'd gone to those summer camps the last few years, the ones offered at the community college? She was here last week after Cecily stopped by, and everyone in town knows that Cecily is trying to get that bill passed to limit yard clutter."

"Garden gnomes aren't exactly campers and boats and huge storage boxes. That's more what she's up in arms about, right? People parking big rigs they're not using and becoming an eyesore."

"That's what's in the bill, but she's also gone on a tirade or two about cluttering a yard with what she calls 'junk.' She doesn't see the whimsy in most garden decor. Not that Hans and Greta are junk," she added. She put him on speaker so she could get the groceries put away. "But she's Kelsey's grandmother, and maybe it's a kid's way of showing Grandma that she might be taking things too far. I don't know Cecily well, but she does go off the deep end a bit when she's on a tear."

"You're not wrong, but would Kelsey be able to make the photos look this good?"

"I taught myself a whole lot of stuff to make presentations in Cleveland," she told him. "I took some courses in college, but technology is always changing. Doing this kind of thing is a lot easier than it was twenty years ago if you have the right software." She put away the yogurt and eggs and closed the fridge. "I'm not saying it was her, but it's a possibility I hadn't considered until now. Maybe she feels like her grandmother is wrong."

Greg didn't sound easily convinced. "But if she likes Julian, even just as a friend, wouldn't she know how he feels about them? About the gnomes?"

"Because thirteen-year-old boys are so good at sharing their feelings?"

He laughed softly. "I get your point. But I'm still going to ask to check the Tinsdales' camera feed tonight. Just in case. See you at the game."

Debbie pulled into the school parking lot twelve minutes later. The first person she spotted was her future neighbor, Cecily Markham Haygood, clutching a clipboard and getting people to sign a petition to limit big rig parking in residential spaces.

A part of her wanted to sidestep the encounter, but the entrance to the baseball field made that impossible. She grabbed her warm jacket and headed for the bleachers.

"Debbie!" Cecily met her halfway. "Would you be willing to sign this petition to push the zoning committee to reestablish rules on parking oversized vehicles and trailers in people's yards?"

Debbie put her off. "I've got to give it some consideration before signing, Cecily. I know you can appreciate that. What if people can't afford to park things off-site? Or can't afford to rent a spot? That creates a hardship, doesn't it?"

Cecily held up a laminated montage of pictures. Each photo featured an oversized camper, commercial rig, or boat parked in close quarters to their neighbor's property. "I'm not talking unreasonable here," she told Debbie. "Or regular-sized things. I'm talking the mammoth things that a lot of people are buying these days. When people with small building lots park ginormous things in their driveways, it creates two significant problems. An eyesore, and a traffic hazard. A lot of these people can't even see around them to pull out of their driveways safely. That should be a consideration before they buy boats or campers or buildings that overpower their space. If we make it a law, then the RV stores and the like will have to inform people if the rig is too big to park on a small lot. I think that's just the common sense of the situation."

Looking at the photos, Debbie couldn't disagree.

Cecily seized the moment. "I'm not asking them to ban RVs and boats and work trucks. But part of a buyer's expectation should include considering where they're going to park it or store it if it's oversized. That's what I want the zoning committee to reexamine. Items over a certain size should have to be parked or stored in a place that doesn't interfere with public safety."

"What about the people who already have those items? What kind of provision are you thinking for that?" Debbie asked. "Will the town grandfather them in? Or make them toe the line instantly?"

"My suggestion would be a time frame," Cecily replied. "Give them twenty-four months to make arrangements or budget accordingly." She proffered the clipboard and a pen.

Debbie didn't take either. "I have to do a little more digging, Cecily. I mean, how big a problem is this, really?"

Cecily answered quickly. "Big enough that Jake Abrams's eight-year-old son nearly got hit by a car two weeks back because the driver never saw the little guy on his bike until the last moment." There was no doubting the sincerity in the woman's gaze. "The neighbor's massive RV blocking his view left the driver with a very small window of time to react. Even going slow, it wasn't enough.

Brody escaped unharmed but the bike was totaled, and that's too close in my opinion."

Debbie winced. "I heard about the accident but not about the details."

"It's not about aesthetics, although that shouldn't be ignored. I know what people say." Cecily shrugged one shoulder. "Some people think that because I do a gardening talk show about keeping yards neat and tidy, I'm trying to push my ideas of what's good and bad on everyone, but that's not the case. It's safety, Debbie."

"Is the boy okay?"

"This time, yes. But that accident was what pushed me to start the petition. Brody got away with nothing but some scrapes on one leg. He dove to the side and ditched the bike. The driver was going slowly, looking for an address. If she'd been doing thirty miles an hour, the outcome could have been a lot worse. As it is, the woman was distraught by what happened."

"Of course she was. Who wouldn't be?"

"Exactly."

This new information put the petition in a new light. Debbie reached for the pen and signed. Then she faced Cecily. "I'm not the type to worry about what a person does or doesn't put in their yard," she told her. "But that could be because I've never lived next to or across from anything objectionable. I can see how something like this camper or that monster boat makes it impossible for drivers to see who might be coming out of either of these driveways. And that's not good."

"Thank you!" Cecily nodded. "I know I'm kind of a stickler about keeping up appearances, but it's not like I expect fancy. We're not a fancy kind of place, but we are a *good* place, and I think it's important to keep it that way."

"On that we can agree."

As Debbie moved to one side to walk away, Cecily's grand-daughter hopped out of a car.

A gray car, not too big.

Her mother was behind the wheel. She rolled down her window and called out to them. "Can't stay for the game. Dean is putting new brakes on my car, so I borrowed one from his stash of vehicles, but I've got to get it back. Another customer needs it for the night."

Dean Addison kept a couple of vehicles on hand in case his customers needed transportation while he worked on their cars. They were nothing fancy, but they served the purpose. It was a big help to people in a small town.

Kelsey headed toward the baseball field. "Hey, Grandma! Hey, Debbie!" She flashed them both a quick smile as she hurried to the fence around the diamond, a small bag slung over her shoulder.

"Have you got a warm-enough coat, honey? I've got one of my big, roomy sweatshirts in the car," Cecily told her, but Kelsey waved her off.

"I'm fine. I'm taking pictures, so I'll be moving around. But thank you!"

Debbie followed her to the field.

The game had started while she was talking to Cecily. Greg spotted her and met her halfway to the bleachers. She hugged him, and he hugged her right back. "I could get used to this." He pulled back, caught her eye, and winked. "And I'm mighty glad to get the chance, Future Mrs. Connor."

"Me too. Speaking of Mr. and Mrs., I set up a tasting for Sunday afternoon. Two different places. They do on-site weddings and catering, so that keeps our options open. Your mom said she'd make Sunday dinner for the boys."

"Great. Except that's your only day off. Are you sure you want to spend it tasting food? Couldn't we just order takeout from both places and do our own comparison?"

"That sounds delightfully easy, doesn't it? Here's the problem, though. Their restaurant menus aren't the same as their catering menus, so even if the takeout's top-notch, the catering might not be what we're after. If it wasn't for my frugal nature, I'd just sign off on a venue with food and check the whole thing off my list," she confessed. "But I can't justify that kind of expense. Who ever said planning a wedding is fun?" She leaned her head against his chest and took a deep breath. "Because it's not."

His arm tightened around her. "Let me help. There's a lot I can do with a few phone calls, honey. Let me check some things off your list."

It was a great offer. But… "I'd love your help, but I also know you're booked solid with work. Your day goes hours later than mine. My problem is that I have Monday afternoons pretty free, but a lot of venues and places don't have the right staff on Mondays. That means I'm running into conflicts. The rest of my week is busy. Tell me again why we didn't just elope right after that beautiful Valentine's Day proposal?"

He laughed. "Because we have two boys and family and friends who would be highly insulted if we did that. But if that's what you want, we'll do it. I don't want to dump all this on you. No one needs the extra stress."

She leaned back and looked up at him then raised her hand and touched his face. "No eloping."

"And can I convince you to stop worrying about money?" He posed the question sincerely, and she loved him for it.

"You can try, but it won't work," she replied honestly. "Being careful with finances is a quality you and I share. But I'm determined to have this settled over the next few weeks. That's my goal. If nothing else, I do have a dress. Which reminds me, have you and the boys chosen your suits?"

He winced. "Not yet. I was going to take them shopping on Saturday, but they rescheduled Jaxon's game for noon, so there might not be time."

"Translation: the last thing you want to do is go suit shopping at the mall after spending hours at a baseball game." She chuckled. "They're your best men. I think we've got to make them feel like it, don't we? Without a crazy bachelor party, of course."

He laughed. "Spare me that. Then yes, I'll take them shopping after the game. We can shower and hit the stores in New Philadelphia by late afternoon. How hard can it be?"

"Hard enough you might want me or your mother with you."

He started to say something, paused, and then said, "I think you're right. A woman's perspective would be good. Can we make it a family trip? You, me, and the boys?"

"Will having me there crowd them?"

Greg shook his head. "A year ago I might have said yes, but I think they're getting used to you now." He winked, teasing. "It could be your wonderful personality or that you have a knack for loving them unconditionally, but I actually think it was your breakfast sandwiches that tipped the scales."

She laughed. "I do make a mean breakfast sandwich, and my chicken parm is to die for. Have you told them about Hans?"

"No time. I'll tell them on the way home. At least with Greta back, it looks less like theft and more like a kid's prank. That doesn't make it right, but it does make it better."

The stands erupted just then. They turned in time to see Julian leap into the air, snag a line drive, then throw the ball to first base. The runner on first got caught between bases, and in a span of tight, terse seconds, Julian and the first baseman were able to tag him out, ending the inning.

Greg fist-pumped the air. "Yes! Great play, guys!"

Half the bleachers agreed. The parents from the visiting team looked less enthralled, and when Julian's team won with a decisive six to three score, the Claymont side cheered. And there, on the lower branches of a big Norway maple tree, was Kelsey Addison, taking pictures, presumably for the eighth-grade yearbook.

The yearbook, Debbie had heard, wasn't a fancy hardbound edition like the high school version. It was more of a class project like the recipe books local churches loved to compile as fundraisers.

Kelsey looked content up there on her branch. As if she knew what she needed for a good photo shoot and was willing to do what it took to get it done. Was that because she'd beaten a life-threatening disease at a young age and had a heightened appreciation for life? Or was she just a kid that liked to excel?

Either way, she'd become a good friend to Julian. Unless she was the one who'd taken Greta, returned her, and had now taken Hans.

Kelsey swung down out of the tree as the players left the field to stow the equipment in the nearby shed. "Hey. Julian!"

He turned when she called his name. "Yeah?"

She patted the bag at her side. "I got some great shots. Of the whole team. I'll send them to you later. Okay?"

"Yeah." One single word, but Debbie recognized the expression on his face.

Greg's younger son was smitten.

She didn't know if Kelsey felt the same way, and they'd gone up and down a few roller coaster rides with Jaxon as he'd matured the past couple of years. She hadn't been around kids or teens in a long time, but she'd learned a lot as Jaxon went through a few tough life lessons. Enough that she would be better equipped to handle the same kind of things with his younger brother.

CHAPTER NINE

*J*ulian jumped out of Greg's truck before it came to a complete stop as Greg parked in the turnaround. He rushed to his left. "You're right! She's back! And someone did take Hans! What's going on around here?"

Jaxon crossed the yard at a more even pace. "Somebody's having a whole lot of fun. They could've just asked. It's probably that girlfriend of yours. She's always doing some fancy stuff on her tablet. She knows what she's doing too."

Brows drawn, Julian said, "I don't have a girlfriend."

"Right." Jaxon rolled his eyes as he bent forward. He lifted Greta, turned, and frowned. "Julian, look."

Debbie followed the direction of their gazes as Greg came their way.

"Her foot's still messed up," Jaxon said.

"It is." Julian stared at the gnome. "How can that be?"

"Clever computer skills," said Debbie. Greg stretched a hand out for the braided blond gnome as she spoke.

"Hand her over," he told Jaxon. "I'm going to take care of that right now. Then no one has to photo-fix anything."

The state of her foot had made Julian frown. Greg's decision to fix the gnome wiped the frown away. "I'll do dishes tonight, Dad. I don't mind."

Greg and the boys had taken turns with kitchen duty since the boys got old enough to do it properly. That made it a three-day rotation, and today, if Debbie's calculations were correct, was Greg's day. He palmed Julian's head as he headed for his work area in the back of the double-wide garage. "I'd appreciate it."

They had a simple sandwich supper, and all seemed well. Mostly well. Even with Hans gone, a calm had descended. Maybe because if Greta was returned, it was a reasonable assumption that Hans would be too. Julian had just finished loading the dishwasher when his laptop buzzed a notification. He swiped the screen, then whistled softly. "Man. She's good."

Debbie had finished wiping the table and the nearby countertop. She rinsed the dishcloth and tossed it into the laundry basket. "Who's good?"

"Kelsey. Check these out."

Debbie leaned over his shoulder. A series of images dominated the screen. They were baseball photos the girl had shot that afternoon. "That's a quick turnaround. She must have sent them right over."

"Not just that." Julian scrolled to the next screen. "Look what she did with them. The first ones are the original pictures. The second set are the ones she played with."

Debbie leaned closer to peruse the shots.

Not only did Kelsey have a good eye, but she understood the importance of a strong vantage point. She'd worked at the top of the bleachers, then from the tree to the far right of the field and used the tree's angle and height to get impressive shots. It was good stuff.

But what caught Debbie's eye were the graphics Kelsey made from the photos. She'd shaded some things, blurred others, brought things forward, and altogether had come up with great effects that showed the well-done photos in a whole new light.

It wasn't just good work for a fourteen-year-old. It was great work by any standard, and it solidified a possibility to Debbie.

Kelsey Addison might be behind the missing lawn ornaments that were showing up on social media. Her technique was plenty good enough to do it. That put Julian's friend and Cecily's granddaughter at the very top of the suspect list.

The essence of calm lasted all of ninety minutes. Then Janet called Debbie's phone. "Check the town's website. You're not going to believe what I'm seeing."

Debbie scrolled to the social media feeds embedded in Dennison's homepage. It seemed Tucker had shared some of NoPlaceLikeGnome's posts. As she found the images, she heard the boys' phones chime with incoming text notifications.

Hans was doing battle.

The gnome was standing his ground against three fairly wild-looking metal leprechauns in multiple locations around their sleepy little town. The Celtic trio were the kind of lawn ornaments that were soldered onto a metal stick. That made them easy to poke into the ground. They also would have been popular around St. Patrick's Day. Did that mean the threesome was stolen weeks before?

Debbie had no idea, but the photography was certainly clever and fun. It was set up as a three-on-one skirmish as the trio of rowdy leprechauns were positioned on all sides of the stalwart little gnome.

"I'm not sure this is a fair fight." Debbie said the words out loud even though she knew she was referring to inanimate objects that couldn't actually wage war. "There are three of them and one Hans.

At least they're all about the same size," she went on as Julian scrolled his phone.

Three of the five pictures matched the geographic areas that the thief had posted with Greta the week before. Two were different. One was done by the old industrial buildings flanking the once-thriving railroad tracks. The last image of the skirmish was done right outside of the town hall.

In front of Ian's office.

The upgraded parts of town gleamed in these new pictures, and the poster hadn't just filled the new roadside urns with gorgeous flowers. He or she had filled the hanging baskets above. Where people had purchased space to have a banner of a military family or friend waving in the April through October breezes, the poster had created medieval style banners of Hans, looking almost fierce—in a comical way—as the battle with the real Hans ensued below. Across the bottom was this single line. *"I will find you, my love. And we shall enjoy pasta from Buona Vita beneath the moon and stars."*

"Man. This guy's good," Julian said.

"Or girl," Jaxon added. When Julian muttered something under his breath, Jaxon shrugged. "I'm just saying that Kelsey knows what she's doing around photo software. She's been doing it long enough. She was at the same camp I was at five years ago," he reminded Julian. "Only I was ten, and she was seven. She was still better than me."

Julian gulped hard. He didn't seem to know what to say or do. Then he spoke. "She wouldn't do this without telling me."

Jaxon didn't seem so sure, but Debbie agreed with Julian out loud, even if she had her own doubts about Kelsey. "Your brother has a good point," she said.

Greg had finished mending Greta's foot in the garage. He came into the room as they continued the discussion. Debbie handed him her phone so he could see the topic of conversation, and he whistled softly.

"The pictures she did of the game show some mad skills," Debbie said.

Jaxon grinned. "It's funny to hear you use words like 'mad skills.'"

She laughed. "Hey! I'm not *that* old," she teased. "But even with Kelsey's talent and skill, I can't imagine her taking Hans or Greta from the yard. Even if she did, that wouldn't explain the leprechauns and the sign that went missing from Patricia Franklin's place. Plus, those brightly painted wooden flowers came from somewhere."

"I'm going to ask her." Julian stood. He set his shoulders back and looked very determined.

"Might not want to do that," advised Jaxon. "Girls don't like being accused of things."

"Well, she was here the night Greta disappeared, and she didn't get to today's game until it started. That was over an hour after school."

Julian's tone insinuated that the teenage girl might have been already tried and convicted in his head, so Debbie raised a hand of caution. "Was she in school today?"

Julian nodded. "Yeah. We have history together."

Debbie gently pointed out the needed timeline. "Then would she have had time to take Hans, take all those pics, and edit them together?" She was doing the math for herself as much as for Julian. She pointed to the pictures on the phone and arched an eyebrow in question. "And despite her skills, doing this kind of thing isn't an instant fix, even with great software. She would have had to come to your game, get back home, tweak your pictures, and send them to you. Then get these pictures of Hans posted and tag the town's account."

"I don't think any mere mortal could do that." Jaxon examined the pictures on his phone again. "But whoever did these pics with Hans is good. Like, legit good."

"Where do you think the leprechauns came from?" Julian wondered.

Debbie shrugged. "I have no idea, but my guess is, now that they're being shared, someone will notice them missing. I expect we'll find out where they belong pretty quickly. But the real question here is…" She lifted her phone. "Who will emerge triumphant?"

"Hans, of course." Julian spoke immediately. "The underdog always wins in the end."

"I agree." Jaxon fist-bumped his younger brother and stood. "Leprechauns have their place, but I'm pretty sure Hans can stand his ground. He might be small, but he's mighty. And he's got a girl to come home to. That makes a difference."

Greg met Debbie's eyes across the room. Then he winked and smiled, and she knew what he meant. Having a girl—or boy—to come home to did make all the difference. Or at least for her and Greg, it would soon, once they were married.

The battle raged for several more days.

The artist didn't post often, but each update demonstrated the ongoing skirmish between the leprechauns and Hans. Short, pithy statements accompanied the amusing graphics.

There were montages of leprechauns hunting through dense woods. They weren't really woods. The shots were compiled in what appeared to be a brushy lot just east of the depot. Staged properly, the leprechauns appeared to be scouting dense vegetation, to no avail.

There were over-the-top intense pictures of Hans, scanning the town from high vantage points, weighing his options as the trio of green metallic leprechauns strategized in the distance.

And then there were images of Hans meeting with a duo of wizened old gnomes that looked like they were taken from Silas Thumm's place that backed up to McClusky Park. The aged gnomes bore the scars of years of use, but the artist made them look less battle-weary in the depictions. Using few words and exaggerated expressions, Debbie saw it was clear the aged gnomes were on Hans's side.

Despite the clear-cut thievery—or probably because the thief had already returned a few of the things he or she had taken—the series of photographic story-telling clips had caught what seemed like the whole town's attention. By Sunday afternoon the ongoing saga had been shared hundreds of times, and people across Ohio were watching to see what would happen next and who would win.

But more important than following the story, to Debbie anyway, was wedding planning. While Paulette made dinner for the boys that night, Debbie and Greg tasted possible food choices for their wedding.

Both venues were lovely. And pricey. And the samples were fine. But as they left the second venue, Debbie sighed.

Greg reached around her to open the car door for her. "Not a fan?"

"Both were good," she said as she climbed into her seat. "But not memorable."

"Honey, we know most of the same people. I'm not sure that memorable is the adjective they'd use for dinner." He held her gaze, and his eyes twinkled at hers. "Filling. Delicious. Great! *Mangia!*" He threw out the Italian term with a grin. "But I'm pretty sure—"

She put her hand on his arm. "Wait. Stop. You've got it. Greg, you're a genius! I can't believe I didn't think of this before. Buono Vita!"

"Your favorite Italian restaurant. Except they're a dine-in place, they don't cater, and they're too small for our families and friends. So that knocks them out of the running, doesn't it?"

Debbie wasn't so sure. "Maybe? But what's the harm in asking?" She didn't try to hide the excitement in her voice. "I'll go see them after work tomorrow."

"Tuesday," Greg reminded her. "They're not open on Monday."

"Then I'll call and leave a message," she replied. "I know they're technically closed on Monday, but I also know that's when they do all the quiet work. Deep cleaning, ordering, organizing. Ricky always told me that Sunday is for rest. Monday is for prep. The worst he can say is no."

He didn't say no when he replied to her message on Monday.

In fact, he sounded so happy to be asked that Debbie was pretty sure that if she won the lottery, she wouldn't be happier than knowing the guys had gotten their suits, she had her dress, alterations were being done, and they'd have food.

At that point, everything else was secondary, other than finding a place to hold the reception, and for the first time since sitting down with Greg in late February to start planning their wedding, she felt like she could breathe. It was a wonderful feeling.

She was on her way to pick up a prescription for her dad when she spotted Bernice's old Chevy wagon pulled up to the curb around the corner from the pharmacy. The car had seen better days decades ago, but it was still running, probably thanks to Dean Addison's mechanical prowess. As Debbie neared the pharmacy lot's entrance, Bernice was sorting through a pile of random cast-off belongings that someone had put at the curb.

There were curb pickups in Cleveland, she recalled from her years in the city. Dumpster divers too. People who hunted up anything of value to make ends meet or just for the fun of it. As she signaled her turn into the lot, she saw Bernice stand upright and emerge triumphant from the pile.

In her hands she held lawn ornaments: two garish flamingos and an oversized pinwheel. The pinwheel was a seventies throwback, quite retro, done in tie-dyed neon shades of pink, yellow, green, and blue. Items firmly in hand, Bernice hurried to her car and carefully placed everything into the back seat.

Debbie called Janet from the parking lot a moment later. "I just spotted Bernice scavenging for yard ornaments at the curbside here by the pharmacy. If we suddenly see flamingos or a pinwheel flower showing up in the posts, we'll know who our perp is!"

"That's so weird." Janet huffed a breath. "Why is she doing this? She's quirky, but stockpiling random yard ornaments seems out of character to me. And she hasn't said another word about the cat, and he's still here."

"I don't doubt her cat efforts at all." Debbie opened her door as she spoke. "She's got a way with them, and I'm sure she'll catch our lurker before long. But the yard stuff *is* weird. What's an old woman, living alone, doing with all the stuff she's collecting? It's odd, isn't it? The last time we dealt with a collector, she had specific reasons for what she was doing."

"Well." Janet let the single word hang on its own, then continued. "It's Bernice. She marches to a different drummer. I'm about to call a 'lid' on Easter orders," she added in a shift of subject. "I think we've got all we can handle for a Holy Saturday pick up. The phone's been ringing off the hook this afternoon, and I don't want to promise more than I can deliver."

"Sounds good. I wanted to be at the Good Friday prayer service with Greg and the boys, so it's better if we don't overbook. Uh-oh. Wait a minute." She'd been moving toward the pharmacy, but she paused when a small gray car pulled into the pharmacy parking lot. It was silly, of course. The sheer number of gray cars made it unlikely to spot a specific one, but a lot of the local gray automobiles were big SUV types. This one wasn't big.

But when she spotted Rhonda Bontrager getting out of the passenger side of the car, she shrugged it off, because she was pretty sure the Mennonite woman wasn't running around pilfering from people's yards and posting on social media.

"I stop every time I see a small gray car," she confessed to Janet as she moved toward the store again. Bernice had started her car and was pulling away from the corner as Debbie reached the door. "As if someone driving a small gray car is going to be wearing a sign saying 'I'm the gnome thief' or some such thing. At least we know whoever it is returns things after a while."

"It's strange and a little funny," agreed Janet. "Not at first, but it's kind of amazing to see their knack for visual storytelling."

"A picture's worth a thousand words. I should go. I'm in the store."

"Bye!"

Debbie tucked the phone into her purse as she returned to pondering Bernice's actions.

She didn't know the elderly woman very well. Not like Janet and Greg did. But between the information she'd gleaned from Greg about the big stash of yard ornaments in Bernice's garage and the actions she'd just witnessed, she realized Bernice might not be doing anything wrong—but she did seem to be acting out of character at the very same time that odd things were disappearing around the town.

The thought of her creating and posting the story vignettes being shared online didn't seem likely, but she had the time and the proclivity to gather things of interest that could be involved.

Was she helping someone else? Knowingly or inadvertently?

Debbie couldn't be sure either way, but she wasn't blind to the possibility. If someone was taking advantage of an older woman, then the town had a potentially serious situation on their hands. But who would do that? And why?

It was a question Debbie couldn't answer.

CHAPTER TEN

Rhonda was leaving the prescription counter as Debbie approached it. She almost passed by, but Debbie called her name softly. When she turned, Debbie said, "Hi, Rhonda, I'm Debbie, from the café. How's your husband doing? Are things improving? My mom was asking after him yesterday afternoon."

Rhonda nodded as Debbie posed the question. "Better, ja. Not *gut*, not yet, but better. Day by day, you know? And your *maam*, she is a kind person. Tell her thank you for asking."

"I will," Debbie promised. "She'll be glad to hear it. I was hoping to make the drive up to your shop after Easter to look at swings. Greg and I decided that a pretty swing would be our wedding present to ourselves. I think I'd like a sweetheart swing, like my parents got from you two years ago. If you have any in stock, that is."

At first Rhonda seemed hesitant, but then she took a breath and her expression eased. "We have some, ja. It is a good time to get them, before people come looking. Once tourist season comes around, things sell quick."

"That'll start soon."

Rhonda bobbed her head. "That is our busy time. From May through December. December is when we finish up, when so many come for the Journey to Bethlehem in Walnut Creek, but we are well-stocked now. Ephraim made many swings over the winter before his surgery. There are a dozen or more and some with those nice hearts. I think you will find what you want."

"Good!" Debbie flashed her a bright smile. "I wanted to get one early enough in spring to enjoy it all season. I'll drive up and see you soon."

"Auntie?"

Rhonda turned. So did Debbie.

A thirtysomething man came their way. He raised a small paper bag in his right hand. "I realized I was running low on a few things back at the house, so I figured I'd run in and get them. Uncle Ephraim was fine with it, but I think the physical therapy tired him out. He looks fatigued. Hello." He turned to Debbie as he finished what he was saying. "I'm Rhonda's nephew. Ben."

She extended her hand quickly. "Debbie Albright. Whistle Stop Café."

"The amazingly delicious cookies from last week." He lifted both brows in appreciation as Rhonda darted a look his way.

"Of course your uncle is worn out." She spoke in a hurry, under-standably. "We must go. We must get him home to rest. I know this," Rhonda added, as if scolding herself.

Debbie agreed. "I don't want to keep you. Either of you. I'll be by to pick out that swing later this month, Rhonda."

Rhonda hurried out of the store, clearly worried.

Pastor Nick called Debbie a few minutes later. She took the call as she was pulling into her parents' driveway to drop off her dad's new allergy medication. "Pastor, hello. I expect you're still wondering about a wedding date, right?"

He chuckled. "We're not that busy that we can't accommodate two of my favorite people. No, I'm calling because you and Janet volunteered to deliver Easter lilies to people to let them know all are welcome in our community. I wanted to make sure it was still all right and fill you in on this week's details."

"We're glad to do it," she assured him. The church had decided to gift lilies to various people throughout the town as a simple way to reach out and say, "Happy Easter."

"The lilies are scheduled to arrive at the church on Wednesday morning," he told her. "We'd like to get them all delivered by Thursday afternoon so we don't have anything taking time away from the Maundy Thursday service or the Good Friday remembrance. Does that work for you and Janet?"

"Just fine," she told him. "Can we come get ours after we close up the café on Wednesday? Then we can head out and deliver them. There's a better chance of catching people home a little later in the day."

"That's perfect. We'll see you then. Thank you so much."

"Glad to help."

When she arrived, no one was home at her parents' house. Her father had his weekly golf outing tonight, and her mother had taken an extra shift at the medical office, so she dropped off the small bag and started back toward her place.

Then she glanced at her watch. She was earlier than she'd expected to be, so she decided to do a little drive around town. She went up one street, then down another just to see what kind of lawn ornaments were prevalent. When she was done with her self-guided tour, she was more than a little surprised.

She'd lived in a high-rise in Cleveland. Her job had been on the upper floor of a downtown office building. Lawn statues and ornaments weren't commonplace. In fact, in the business area, they were nonexistent. But here, in the heart of Dennison, they were everywhere.

Short, white picket fencing was huge, but so were wooden flowers, pinwheels, garden statues, wishing wells, wheelbarrows, flags, fairy houses, and garden spikes of all kinds. Some held signs, some sported woodland creatures, and she even spied a couple of those saucy green leprechauns. Wooden and resin farm animals found their way into multiple spring garden settings, but there were also stoneware rabbits, woodchucks, and birds.

She stopped by Janet's house before she went home. "I had no idea our town embraced so much yard decor. How have I missed this?" she asked.

Janet laughed. "Twenty years in the city will do that," she replied. "It's gotten to be a thing."

Debbie whooshed out a breath. "Is it overdone, do you think? I mean, I thought the cute things my mom gave me were just darling…"

"The cute wooden things that Ray Zink made in his garage before going into assisted living and selling you the house?"

"Yes. I love them. Partially because they're so nicely done and partly because Ray made them. I guess I never noticed how prevalent these kinds of things are."

"Dani Addison is even doing a series of early spring craft classes to help people make their own garden decor. That way they can paint things whatever color balances or complements their yard scheme."

Debbie had been about to take a sip from a water bottle. She paused. "Yards have schemes?"

"And themes," Janet added, then laughed at Debbie's expression. "Most just want to add a blast of color to their landscaping because perennials go in and out of bloom and annuals get pricey to replace every year. Yard ornaments have gotten to be a thing. Though they're not cheap," she added. "My neighbor paid nearly sixty dollars for those two stoneware rabbits she has peeking out of her hostas."

"They're only this big." Debbie formed her hands into a small oval, and Janet nodded.

"Yes, but they're made of molded concrete. They'll last forever, and they'll never blow away."

Debbie wasn't sure she'd care enough about anything in a garden to want it to last forever, but at least the longevity made the cost less daunting. "I guess I was too busy setting things up for my house, then the café, to notice this last year. To think it took someone taking things from this yard and that to even put it on my radar."

"Romance and work are pretty strong distractions." Janet winked and waved at her neighbor's home. "Hettie Jackson takes this craze to new heights. She's got a different display for every month from Valentine's Day on. It's gotten to be like living in a calendar layout with each month prettier than the last. She retired early and has no desire to go down South in the winter. She says she likes looking out and seeing pretty things and it simply makes her love her home more each year."

"Can't fault that. We get enough months of gray, brown, and white, so if that helps her deal with winter, it makes sense to me."

"That's where Hettie is different from so many," Janet went on. "She claims she *doesn't* deal with winter. Or ice, or snow, or sleet. She says she embraces it, and that has made all the difference."

Debbie looked at Janet and grinned. "I love that."

Janet high-fived her. "Me too. She's got the right attitude for a Northern woman. If you can't change it, deal with it. With a smile," she added.

Debbie headed for Greg's house. The boys both had practice today, then single games tomorrow after school and no games over Easter weekend. The combination of a much-appreciated window of time and good weather inspired her to get some more done on those front borders. She put her signal on as she approached the driveway, made the turn, and hit the brakes hard.

The gardens were cleaned out.

Totally cleaned out.

Instead of random, crowded sprouts of invasive weeds and perennials running amok, the three distinct borders were now neat and clean, as if they'd been professionally excised by the nice landscaper whose estimate had been way more than they wanted to spend.

Debbie swallowed hard, parked, got out of the car, and approached the front of the house.

The gardens weren't simply weeded.

They were lovely.

She could see where the soil had been turned over along one edge and there, neatly planted or transplanted along each expanse, were the original perennials that Holly Connor had planted over a decade ago. A few small bushes formed the backdrop near the house. From there, the borders fanned out with clumps of artfully arranged plants, none of which Debbie recognized. Despite that, the clumps looked happy and healthy, and that in itself was a big change.

She hauled in a deep breath and called Greg. He was scheduled to pick up both boys from practice, and he answered quickly. "Hey, darling. What do you need?"

"You hired the landscaper."

"I what?" Surprise hitched his voice up a notch. "We agreed not to, right? That we'd muddle along and get things done over the next month or two."

"That's what we said, but I'm looking at a beautifully landscaped bunch of borders, and if you weren't here doing it—"

"I can confirm that I absolutely was not," he assured her.

"And it wasn't me or Janet, because we were both working all day, then—" She paused as she spotted something on the front door.

She crossed the walkway, barely daring to believe her eyes, and untaped the business-sized white envelope. She opened it and slipped out a two-page note tucked inside.

You have been visited by the Dennison Weed Stealers Society. This visit was coordinated by people who love, love, love gardens—and really like helping others.

No thanks needed... Weed Stealers are glad to be of service!

Sincerely,

The Weed Stealers of Our Little Town

"What in the world?" Greg sounded as astounded as she felt once she'd read him the note.

"I'm sending you pictures." She stood back and took several quick shots, then sent them to Greg's phone. "And there's a second sheet in the envelope with a garden map. It's a pencil sketch of what the plants are and when they bloom, so we don't pull the wrong things out."

He whistled. "I'm looking at the pictures now. That's incredible. And really pretty."

"I know. I'm staring at this and getting all misty-eyed, because someone—"

"Wait. Are you crying? For real?"

"Not crying exactly, but almost crying," she told him. "And almost doesn't count."

"It is beautiful. They did a stellar job. How can we thank them?" he asked.

"By paying it forward and doing something nice for someone else when they least expect it." She heard shouts as the boys' practices ended. The voices got louder as the boys got closer to the truck. "I'll see you guys in a few minutes. Okay?"

"Yes. Debbie?"

"Yes?"

"I love you."

Oh those words. So simple and sweet. His words, his tone, his manner... The whole thing touched her heart, and in a few months' time they'd be married. Living together. With well-tended gardens.

The thought made her grin.

Greta still looked lonely on her side of the garden, but they had reason to hope that Hans would be returned once his adventures were complete.

She checked the town's social media feeds.

Today's posts included one from area churches listing Easter weekend services, alongside a few posts about spring cleanup dates and upcoming festivals, but nothing about Hans and his three ruddy-haired mischievous friends.

She kind of missed those posts, and the fact that she was looking forward to them made her feel guilty. Because whoever was having sport with the stolen objects was doing it with other people's possessions.

And yet—she *did* miss it. The antics of the yard ornaments made people laugh, and laughing was good.

Greg pulled in a few minutes later.

He climbed out one side of the truck, Jaxon climbed out the other, and Julian hopped out of the back seat. Excitement brought Julian to the front yard at a fast clip. "This looks awesome! Like you can see what's supposed to be here, right? And the ones that are left? Are these all the things my mom planted?" There was no denying the excitement in the teen's face and his voice.

Debbie looked at Greg, and Greg nodded. "Yes. This was her project, and whoever did this had an eye for what was supposed to be here and what wasn't. Just like your mom always did."

Jaxon stared at the gardens. He drew a breath and raised his shoulders. "It looks a lot like back then. Only not too many flowers are blooming."

"They bloom throughout the season," Greg told him. "Some now, some in May, then June, July, and so on, right into fall. And your mom always added some annuals. Flowers that only bloom for a year and then you replace them the next year," he explained when the boys looked blank. "That way there's color all year. And then chrysanthemums every September."

"And we can do that. Right?" Julian wasn't about to be put off.

"Absolutely," Debbie and Greg said together.

"Not for a few weeks yet," Greg added, "because we still get some cold nights, but we can go and see Mrs. Haywood at the nursery and plug a bunch of annuals into the gardens. That brightens things up for the rest of the year."

The boys smiled. Jaxon's was thoughtful, as if seeing the garden cleaned out the way his mother would have done it made him both happy and sad at the same time. Julian's was more ebullient, as if the sheer joy of seeing a partial memory come alive meant a great deal.

Debbie was sure it did. Losing a parent was an awful thing for anyone. The thought of forgetting that parent would be a rough road for any kid.

"I gotta shower." Jaxon headed for the door. "But it sure looks great."

"Me too when he's done." Julian slung his book bag over his shoulder and tucked his mitt beneath one arm. "And can we put lots of colors in when we buy the other flowers, Dad? Like in that picture when I was just a little kid?"

"Wearing that miniature baseball outfit?" asked Greg.

"Yep." Julian grinned. "I looked like a goof because you guys didn't cut my hair, but this garden reminds me of that picture now."

He headed inside, and Greg turned toward Debbie. "Whoever did this touched a lot of hearts today."

"They sure did. And they gave us a blueprint to work with," she told him. "I don't mind playing in the dirt, but I was totally lost about what to do, what to keep, what to pull out. I was thoroughly intimidated by it, so this is a perfect solution. Look." She bent over and moved some of the mulch aside. "There's a weed barrier here. That means we won't have a lot of weeds or things popping through."

"And we can make slits where we want to put the annuals and then reuse those slits each year." Greg made it sound quite reasonable, which it was. Now. It hadn't looked the least bit reasonable the previous day. "Whoever did this had a good heart and knows how to make things as easy as possible."

Debbie couldn't say for sure, but quietly helping and using her knowledge to get things done quickly was right up Cecily Haygood's alley. If she was the one that organized this beautiful restructuring, she was a great neighbor to have close by. And if the ornament thief and story creator turned out to be Cecily's granddaughter Kelsey?

The kid had clearly come by her work ethic honestly, if not the stolen ornaments.

CHAPTER ELEVEN

*D*ebbie and Janet decided to borrow Debbie's mom's SUV to deliver the church's lilies on Wednesday afternoon. When they pulled into the church parking lot, Pastor Nick was just inside the door of the parish center, greeting people as they came by to load up the flowers for their assigned routes.

The church liturgy committee had kept the altar decorations quiet and contemplative during the weeks leading up to Easter. Debbie knew that would continue until Easter Sunday. As she and Janet came down the hall, three women were slipping buckets filled with wild apple blossoms into the kitchen cooler, getting ready for a resplendent Sunday altar. Debbie sighed seeing them. "I love apple blossoms. That blend of pink and white, so delicate, yet strong. They make me happy."

Pastor Nick smiled at her. "They're simple and beautiful, aren't they? Just a bunch of little blossoms on a tree branch, yet rare because they're only around for a few weeks out of the year. Once they're gone, they're gone."

"And no forcing them like a hothouse flower," Debbie replied. "But they're not *just* a flower. They hold what it takes to create fruit. It reminds me of how important it is that tiny seeds and fragile blossoms are the beginnings of so many things we need."

"I like that way of looking at it." The pastor indicated the buckets of apple blossoms with a brief nod. "Those come from what's left of the old Simmons orchard. The trees went wild years back. They make beautiful arrangements, and they blossom for weeks this time of year." They crossed to the table filled with potted Easter lilies labeled *Debbie and Janet.* "They had a wide variety of apple trees, so they blossom at different times. Not far from Claymont Creek Farm."

Janet lifted two pots of white lilies, one in each hand. "Spring speaks to us in a way that's different from every other season." She indicated the beauty of the pristine lilies with a jut of her chin. "I love the colors and majesty of fall, but spring is a healing season. It brings us out of a long winter and into that time of renewal, of grace, of Easter. After a long winter, there is something heartening about new life, rebirth, new leaves."

"Exactly." Debbie exchanged a smile with both of them. "I didn't appreciate that the same way in the city. It's less visible there with the tall buildings and the lake, but here? With the widespread vistas and trees?"

"And gardens," teased Janet, making Debbie laugh.

"Yes, that. It brings it all to mind in a different way. A special way. All the new colors, the baby leaves, the bright blossoms, the green grass. It doesn't just bring hope." She angled one plant into the crook of her arm. "It brings joy."

"Amen to that." The pastor helped them load the car, and within minutes they had arrived at their first stop.

Janet aimed a bright smile at the elderly woman whose home overlooked Claymont Creek. "Happy Easter, Florence! A little gift for you from Faith Community Church."

"For me?" Florence Millsap put her hand to her chest, and the look of sheer delight warmed Debbie's heart. "But I don't even go there, girls. I think you have the wrong house, but they sure are a sight, aren't they?" Her kindly voice was only outdone by the longing in her eyes. She reached out one hand and lightly touched the edge of a leaf. "Easter lilies are so pretty, and stronger than they look. I know that from my gardening days."

"Not the wrong house at all," Debbie assured her. She handed the potted flowers over. "Just a neighborly gesture to wish you the very best Easter Sunday."

Florence's eyes went wide. "For me? Really?"

"All for you," Janet replied. "And we hope you enjoy the flowers."

"Thank you!" Eyes damp, the elderly woman clung to the foil-covered pot like one would a lifeline. "Thank you so much!"

"You're welcome. Happy Easter from Faith Community!" They waved goodbye, got back into the SUV, and made several other deliveries.

"This is the easiest job ever." Janet said as they were leaving their ninth delivery. Three small children had been so excited to see their mom get flowers that they danced around the yard in glee. "Spreading joy is wonderful."

"It is. And it's contagious," Debbie added. "Going home on Monday, seeing what someone had done to make my life easier, meant so much to all of us. All I want to do now is share that kindness with others. And—"

She hit the brakes. Not hard, just a quicker-than-usual slowdown because there, in front of them, just beyond the railroad tracks, was Bernice, and she was carrying a very unhappy cat.

The light squeal of the brakes caught Bernice's attention. She looked up and spotted them. She didn't yell, but she carefully mouthed the word "Help!"

That was enough for Debbie and Janet.

Debbie angled the SUV to the curb quickly and hopped out of the car. "How can we help? Do you want me to take him?"

She hoped the answer was no, because the angry cat didn't look like he'd be pleased with a transfer of possession. Sure enough, Bernice shook her head. "My car. Right there. Cat carrier in the back."

Debbie dashed to the old red hatchback while Janet stayed by Bernice. Bernice tried to comfort the cat by whispering to him. "Nice kitty," she murmured. "Sweet kitty. You're so handsome, fellow." She cooed the words in what she probably thought was a cat-friendly voice.

The cat disagreed. As Debbie dashed back with the cat carrier, the cat hissed at Janet, let out a loud and baleful meow, then growled.

"Set it on the ground right there," Bernice instructed Debbie. "Then pinch the latch on the carrier door with two fingers. I'll put him in face first, then I'll close it before he has time to spin around."

Debbie followed the directions and released the latch. The metal door popped open. She pulled it open farther, then held tight.

The orange cat wasn't one bit happy, but as Bernice expertly nudged him head-first into the carrier, Debbie made the door follow the older woman's hand. The firm click when the latch popped into place allowed all three of them to breathe a sigh of relief.

"I'm so impressed that you caught him!" Janet swiped a hand to her brow. "Phew! How did you do that?"

"Food and a frank talking-to, the pair of things that work best when it comes to our feline furry friends." Bernice moved toward the back of her car as she spoke. Debbie followed with the cat tote. She averted her gaze from Janet because it seemed her best friend found the sight of Debbie carrying a very angry cat quite amusing, and Debbie had to fight the urge to laugh herself.

"He took to the food right off," Bernice continued. "And he wasn't averse to the straightforward speech, but he wasn't a fan of being picked up, held, or contained. As you can see and hear."

The yowling cat wasn't afraid to let everyone know how he felt, but he was safe now. Despite the feline's desperate calls, Debbie knew that the cat's future with Bernice and her contacts held better prospects than hunting for scraps along the railroad tracks.

"Do you want him in the hatch area?" she asked, but Bernice shook her head.

"I prefer the back seat so we can wrap a seat belt around the carrier," she replied. "For a fellow that's been striking out on his own for some time, a more cushioned seat is definitely a better choice. Time for our butterscotch friend here to know that life has just taken a more comfortable turn. Besides, I've got a lot of stuff in the hatch area. I've been doing some curb pickups, and there's always a good selection on Wednesdays as people get ready for Thursday trash collection."

"I think the seat belt's a good idea." Debbie leaned in and pulled the seat belt harness from the side of the car. As she leaned over to lock the belt into place, her eyes landed on three items between the back seat and the crowded hatchback of the car. Three green things shoved down and away. Maybe out of sight? Out of mind?

A trio of red-haired metal leprechauns grinned up at her.

She almost said something, but then she caught herself.

Janet had voiced concerns about Bernice and her actions lately. That was enough of a red flag for Debbie, because Janet had known the elderly cat lover for years. Despite that, Debbie didn't believe that Bernice had the internet savvy skills to produce the ongoing story that had been playing out on social media. Janet had shared a similar thought. Still—

The very same leprechauns that were wreaking havoc for little Hans all over social media lay hidden in Bernice's car. Laughing and grinning, each metal fellow featured a slightly different pose. Their different expressions had made it easier for the storyteller to get the most out of each one in his posts.

Her first thought went to Kelsey Addison as she slowly drew back from the car. Kelsey's dad owned the mechanic's garage about five minutes from here. If Kelsey was the artist behind the posts, had Bernice lifted these from the Addisons? Had she stolen Kelsey's props? Or had Kelsey dumped them somewhere to avoid discovery?

Janet took one look at Debbie's face and seemed to realize something was up. She closed the car door and faced Bernice. "Do you need help with him at home?"

Bernice waved that off. "No, although I appreciate the offer. I've got a nice crate all set up for him, litter box and all. A big crate, one of those dog-sized ones. That way he's got room to move but not the freedom to escape. It takes some longer than others to get used to being in a house and being loved on, so I'll give him all the time he needs." She walked around to the front of the car. "That patience has been a big part of my success. I take it one cat at a time," she went on as she swung the driver's door open. "Retraining a cat to love people can take a bit of effort, but it's worth it if it sets them on the right road. If you stay at it long enough, well…" She settled a look of contentment on her very vocal and discontented back seat occupant. "You can truly make a difference."

"And you have. Thank you, Bernice."

Bernice got into the car. She seemed oblivious to the cat's crankiness. When the engine fired up, its noise blocked some of the cat's protests. She pulled away. As soon as she did, Debbie faced Janet. "You're not going to believe what I saw in her car!"

Janet nodded, unsurprised. "The wooden flowers. The ones that were used in Greta's pictures in the park. I couldn't believe it. I saw them through the back window."

Debbie stared at her. "No. Not the flowers. The leprechauns!"

Janet frowned. "The flowers were in the back. Like right on top of other stuff. A red one, an orange one, and two that were bright yellow. Where did you see leprechauns?"

"Between the back seat and the hatch," said Debbie, and she couldn't hide the excitement in her voice. "They were down in that well there. I leaned in to do the seatbelt, and there they were, laughing at me while I'm strapping a very angry cat into place. I was dumbstruck, for real. I didn't know what to say or do, so I finished with the cat and figured we'd talk about it once she was gone. How is she getting these things? And who is she helping?"

"Or…" Janet prefaced her next statement with a sad face. "Who is Bernice stealing from? That might be what we have on our hands, Debbie, and I will be so sad if that's the case. As quirky as Bernice is, she's part of this town. Part of what makes this place special."

Debbie may have been gone for over two decades, but she remembered Bernice from when she was a girl. Janet was right. A friendly town embraced its citizens. They made room for others. The thought that Bernice might not be trustworthy would be a bitter pill for a lot of people to swallow.

Stealing was a crime, not an eccentricity. If that was what she was doing, Ian would have to know. That would be a tough conversation to have.

They delivered the last four potted lilies, but seeing possibly stolen items in Bernice's car had dimmed their enthusiasm. By the time Debbie approached Janet's street, her thoughts weighed heavy. There was no traffic, so she eased over to the side of the road and put the car into park. Then she faced Janet. "I don't know how to handle this."

"Bernice?"

"Yes. It's one thing if she's just snagging things from junk piles. We've all found curbside treasures at one time or another."

Janet seemed doubtful as she shrugged one shoulder. "It's possible. But what's the likelihood that the very same things we know have been stolen are in her car? The leprechauns, plus the flowers."

"I can't help but feel that turning her into the law because we think we saw what *could be* stolen items in the back of her car feels wrong." She took a deep breath. "It feels wrong, even if it's right."

It was a few seconds before Janet responded. "I know. I feel the same way. But what are the odds that she's picked up some of the very things that are being posted as part of the ongoing story this past couple of weeks?"

"Stuff that's been reported missing," added Debbie. "But also we know stuff has been returned, and maybe that's Bernice's part of the scheme. She's on the return committee. That's also possible. Right?"

"It seems about as plausible as anything else we've come up with." Janet gave a half laugh. "Who'd have thought that the missing garden gnome caper might be one of our toughest mysteries yet?"

"Well, that's because it's not normal. For most crimes, big and small, there's a motive and the perpetrator is after something. Cute parodies that tag a small-town social media page aren't going to profit with anything of value. Except laughter."

"And a bunch of locals and nonlocals who cheer every time they get a notification that there's a new Dennison post."

"They say laughter is very therapeutic." Debbie smiled at Janet.

"The best medicine there is. We'll let Ian know because we have to, but he'll be discreet and gentle. He knows Bernice, and he knows the whole town deals with her funny memory and loves her good heart."

"Agreed."

CHAPTER TWELVE

Ian was home when they arrived.

Debbie and Janet exchanged looks once more. "Do we really have to tell him?" Debbie voiced the question, wishing for the response she wasn't going to hear.

"You know we do, but I'll hate doing it." Janet got out of the car. So did Debbie. As they turned to go up the side steps to the house, Debbie paused and pointed west. "Do you see what I see?"

One of Janet's neighbors, Rob Brown, had taken advantage of the lovely evening to do some gardening. He'd trimmed out a vibrant rock garden, bright with spring primroses and a splash of early red and yellow tulips, but that wasn't what captured Debbie's attention.

It was the trio of wooden flowers he'd placed in front of his cream-and-green euonymus bushes. The three brightly painted flowers added a splash of color to the duller-toned shrubs behind them. Although these were all bright yellow, they were exactly like the wooden flowers showing up in the artsy posts. He straightened, noticed them looking, and waved them over.

"What a marvelous afternoon!" he called out as they crossed the street. "I've been waiting for my knees to complain less and the sun to get higher. It turned out today was the day." He smiled as they reached his driveway.

"I love it." Janet swept the yard a look of appreciation. "Well done. Rob, you've met Debbie before, haven't you? At the café?"

"I've had the pleasure of seeing her a time or two." He nodded Debbie's way. "I won't shake hands. Even wearing gloves, my fingers aren't the cleanest at the moment. But my yard's starting to shape up, and that's a good feeling."

"It looks lovely," Debbie told him. "And your grass is such a pretty shade of green. Like Irish green."

"I gave this yard a good raking and fertilizing two weeks back," he told her. "It greened up nice about ten days in, but I didn't have the knee power or stamina to do the clean-out then." He rolled his shoulders as he spoke. "Ground was too cold and wet, but today was perfect. Wasn't it?"

"It sure was." Enthusiasm heightened Janet's agreement. Then she pointed to his wooden flowers. "Those are cute, Rob. Where'd you find them? I don't remember them from last year."

"That Mennonite shop up in Sugarcreek," he said. "The one with the swings and the outdoor furniture. My wife loves that shop."

"Bontrager's."

He nodded. "That's the one. We took a ride up there. Susan likes to have a little bit of fun in the yard. House too, for that matter, but she saw these and said she needed to have them because they're particularly bright. You know how flowers fade here in July and August if it's too hot and dry."

"I sure do," agreed Janet. "Even watering doesn't keep them looking fresh if the sun is too intense."

He nodded again. "That's just what Susan said. She was taken with these because they're not tulips, like so many people use."

That's what had drawn Debbie's attention. A lot of her neighbors put little wooden tulips in their gardens as part of their spring or Easter yard decor every March, but these were different. Bigger, taller, and rounder. Exactly what the poster had used in the social media stories. "More like sunflowers," she noted.

"Good all year," he said. "That's what tipped the scales. That and getting too old to be up and down with too many annuals these days."

"Rob, you know we'd be honored to help whenever you need." Janet put a hand on his arm. "I'm happy to do it. Ian would be too."

His smile said he appreciated the offer. "I'm saving that nice option for when it's absolutely necessary," he told her. "No one wants to be a drain on the neighborhood. If I'm not asking for help all the time, people may be more inclined to help when it's needed. And that way I won't feel like I'm wearing out my welcome."

"Wouldn't happen," Janet assured him.

"Good to hear, but most of us are reluctant to give up that independence we worked so hard to get. For now, these cute flowers liven things up. That's just what Susan had in mind—a splash of color to make people smile. They've got a ton more at the shop." He dabbed an old, thin cotton washcloth to his forehead. "All different colors too, but I gave my wife yellow roses nearly forty-five years ago, and she's been partial to yellow flowers ever since."

His words made Debbie melt. "That's beautiful."

"You ladies have a nice night now."

"We will." They walked back to Janet's house in silence and stayed that way until they were inside.

Ian was in the kitchen. He took one look at the pair of them and sighed.

"What have you two been up to?"

"A soul-stirring delivery service, a surprising find, and an interesting twist," Janet told him.

He held up one finger. "I expect the deliveries were the church's flowers."

"Yes."

"But what about the other two?" he asked as he grabbed a pitcher of tea out of the fridge. "Would you like to join me?"

"I'd love a cold drink." Debbie took a seat at the table.

"Me too." Janet slipped into the chair next to Debbie.

"Glad to oblige." He grabbed a couple of glasses, filled them with ice and tea, and brought them over.

Janet spoke first. "We ran into Bernice not far from the depot."

"Looking for the cat you told her about? I've seen her scouting various areas the past few days. She's been diligent."

"She found him and was carrying him back to the car but definitely needed some help. Which we gave her," said Debbie.

Janet continued the story. "She's got him safe and sound, but when we helped her fasten the cat carrier into her car we discovered a couple of interesting things."

"How interesting?"

Janet lifted one eyebrow. "Possibly misdemeanor-level interesting."

His frown deepened.

"She had three leprechauns in the car," Janet continued. "Debbie saw them when she fastened the seat belt around the carrier."

"I don't know that they're the exact three that have been online," added Debbie. "The ones that went missing from the Calloways' yard, but if they're not the same ones, they were dead ringers for them. They were angled onto the floor between the seats."

"Which is when *I* noticed the flowers in the back of the car," Janet added. "Four bright-toned wooden flowers like the ones that were used in the social media posts about Greta."

"You think Bernice is doing those posts?" Ian didn't bother to soften the incredulous note in his voice. "Have you seen her phone?"

Janet sighed. "Yes and no. Yes, I've seen her phone and no, we don't think she's making the posts. But it's very curious that she's got a stockpile of things at her house..."

That fact made Ian shift both brows up in surprise.

"Boxes and totes and piles of all kinds of garden decor," explained Debbie. "Flowers, animals, fencing. Greg saw it when he was there."

Ian didn't lose the frown. "I know she's been dumpster diving. A lot of people do that or answer curb alerts online so they can pick things up. That's not exactly news."

"Except what would Bernice be doing with so much of it?" Janet posed the question, and Ian shook his head.

"I don't know, but if she's grabbing things off curbs and dumpsters, there's nothing wrong with that. Maybe the person posting dumped the borrowed or stolen flowers and the leprechauns and Bernice inadvertently picked them up. Maybe he or she couldn't get them back to the original owner and didn't know what else to do with them."

"That is a distinct possibility," noted Debbie.

"Then when we pulled in here, we noticed that Rob has been doing yard work today." Janet motioned toward the west-facing window. "Including placing three of those same flowers in his garden. So we walked over to talk to him."

Ian held up his hand. "I'm pretty sure Rob didn't steal anyone's flowers—"

"No, of course not," Debbie said. "He bought them. But he bought them from the very same shop in Sugarcreek that carries the porch swings and the outdoor rockers. All those pretty wooden items."

"Bontrager's."

"Yes!" Now Janet sounded excited. "And who should have stopped by the café this past week, out of the blue, wanting my baked goods and getting into a gray car?"

Ian looked positively stumped. "Everyone in town?"

She laughed. "That's a great answer. No, Rhonda Bontrager. To get cookies, of all things."

Ian didn't seem to find that unusual. "Because your cookies are the best, and she used to come to the Third Street Bakery to buy them. No mystery there."

"She did say they had to bring her husband down here for physical therapy. It's nothing, I'm sure, but it's funny to see her after two years of not seeing her, and then realizing her flowers are in almost all of the social media posts."

"Except that seeing some used ones in Bernice's SUV means they're more common than I would have thought." Debbie pursed her lips. "That kind of blows things wide open again, doesn't it?"

"The mind's a funny thing," Ian told them. He took another swig of his iced tea before continuing. "A lot of stuff goes unnoticed in our everyday lives until something draws our attention to it. Like the flowers Ephraim makes. Or the pinwheels they sell every year at the garden center. They could be in forty or fifty gardens around the county, but we notice them now because whoever is posting and tagging the town's account has brought them to our attention."

Janet sighed. "I have to admit that you're right."

He grinned and raised his glass of tea. "Music to my ears, love."

"Well, since we *have* noticed them and I'm going there next week, I'm going to check them out a little closer. The flowers, I mean. It's a long shot, but if Bontrager's is the source of the flowers, maybe Rhonda will have some insight into this. It can't hurt, right?" Debbie moved toward the door.

Janet followed her and swung the inner door wide. "I'd like to ride along."

Debbie read the look her best friend aimed her way. "We'll double team them."

Janet grinned. "Exactly. I know it's a long shot, but Rhonda's a smart cookie. She might remember something or someone. We're assuming the poster's flowers were stolen, but there haven't been any reports of stolen flowers, right?" She glanced at Ian, and he shook his head.

"Nothing that's come into our office, no."

"I don't want to be a bother with Ephraim on the mend, but maybe our resident storyteller just bought the flowers for his or her tales. The ones we see in the posts look fresh and new."

"Now is when I remind you that Greg had to fix Greta's foot when they got her back because it wasn't actually mended." Ian folded his arms across his middle. "It was doctored by the poster."

"It's still worth a conversation," Janet insisted. "And I might find something I simply have to have in the yard. Plus, Rhonda did get into a gray car."

Ian rolled his eyes. "Whatever is going on, your list of usual suspects is quite unusual this time. Bernice. Rhonda. Tucker. Kelsey. Who, by the way, doesn't drive." He didn't try to hide his doubtful expression. "Good luck with that."

Janet flashed him a saucy smile. "I'll take that wish of good luck. I get to shop and check things out with Debbie. But we'll go soft on Ephraim if he's in the shop."

"I agree." Debbie reached out and gave Janet a quick hug. "We'll draw the line at mild inquisition."

After saying goodbye, Debbie got back into her mother's car and headed for her parents' house. As she parked the SUV alongside her Camry, her phone buzzed a notification. She tapped it open while she was still in the car.

It was a link from a friend. A link that connected her to one of the village's social pages.

An action-packed image of Hans appeared. The gnome looked like he was racing for his life along the tops of the railcars. Focused and intent, the person had made great use of the stationary railcars that were now part of the depot museum. The feisty little gnome brandished a sword scaled to his size. Chin up, he raced across the roofs of the cars, charging forward while the mischievous leprechauns seemed intent on wreaking havoc at the end of the track.

It was clever manipulation. She got out of her mother's car, thinking. Her parents were out to dinner with friends, so she dropped her mother's keys through the old-fashioned mail slot in their front door and drove her own car home.

Janet called before she got there, and Debbie hit the Bluetooth button.

"Did you see the latest installment?" Excitement laced Janet's normally even-toned voice.

"I did." Debbie hesitated before she went further. She'd turned on notifications from the poster's account and the constant dinging of people's reactions meant the followers were growing. "And I expect he or she is getting tons of feedback."

"Lighting up the internet," Janet replied. "Tucker's back in town now. Let's visit him tomorrow afternoon."

"Would Tucker actually do something like this? And if he did, wouldn't he just use his name?"

"Not if he wanted it to have the kind of effect they saw in Texas. Just enough humor to make people laugh and encourage them to click over to the town's pages repeatedly. It's always more fun if it's an anonymous poster or someone using a gag name like this guy. NoPlaceLikeGnome. And if he isn't the one doing it, maybe he can help us figure out who is. Ian says that since it's not really a police matter, he can't launch a full-on investigation. It seems my law enforcement connections don't get us too far in this case, my friend."

Two weeks ago that thought would have filled Debbie with angst. Now?

Not so much. Was that because Greta was returned? Or because she suspected a funny, talented fourteen-year-old girl of being the mastermind and admired her tenacity? That was something she'd have to examine more thoroughly later. "Let's stop by Tucker's office after we close. I know we've got a lot of baking prep to do for Saturday pickups."

"True," replied Janet. "But I've got my baking schedule lined up for tomorrow and Friday. Paulette's coming in early and leaving late, and Charla's coming to help. It's all good. I want to see Tucker's reaction. He's got to be loving this, even if he's not doing it. But if he isn't, he might have an idea who is. Ian said he's in an online photo-editing group and maybe those guys can give us some insight."

"I'm all for that. Oops, getting a call from Pastor Nick. See you in the morning."

"Sounds good!"

Debbie swiped her thumb across the phone screen. Pastor Nick was probably calling people to thank them for their help that day. He was the kind of person that went out of his way to be cordial and appreciative, part of why he was so well loved.

But it wasn't the pastor's voice that greeted her on the other end. It was his wife, Brenda. "Debbie, I know you were here just a few hours ago to pick up flowers, but the strangest thing's happened."

"Strange as in?"

"Your garden statue. The one that's been tearing up the internet?"

"Hans, yes. I saw he was having new adventures today as he raced across the roofs of railcars. He's clearly leading a very active life for a gnome. Someone is very good at creating action out of inaction."

"They sure are," Brenda replied. "Kind of amazing, isn't it? What some people can do with technology? But that's not why I called," she continued. "I called because he was here."

Debbie didn't quite follow. "Who was there?"

"Your little fellow. Hans. He was here, on the church property. I just saw him. It was the oddest thing. I was washing a couple of my bigger kettles, the ones that don't fit into the dishwasher. The big sink overlooks the churchyard around the gazebo. Nick was still working at the church with some people from the liturgy committee, so it was just me on this side of the property. Anyway, I glanced out the window, and there he was. On the steps of the gazebo, standing there as if he was waiting for something."

"Did you grab him?" Debbie asked. This was the first actual sighting of the gnomes in action since the random yard ornaments began disappearing.

"No." Regret deepened Brenda's voice. "I got a call from the hospice house over in Uhrichsville and had to get the message to Nick right away. By the time I got to the side yard the gazebo was empty. He was gone. Nowhere to be seen. I didn't see anyone around or hear any cars taking off."

"Someone on foot, then?"

"Maybe," Brenda said, "but you'd think I'd see them if they were moving around back there, messing with a gnome. But it would be easy for someone to slip away between a house or two. Small yards have that distinct advantage."

"So whoever was there was able to disappear pretty quickly."

Brenda sighed. "I guess they must have, Debbie. It was just getting dusk too. Not dark but not light either."

Debbie didn't know if she should laugh or sigh too. "Brenda, my guess is that if we give it a few days, we'll find out exactly what Hans was doing at the church gazebo. Some epic battle or grand gesture, no doubt."

She was relieved when Brenda laughed. "I expect you're right. Nick and I both get a kick out of these little vignettes they keep posting. Are your boys okay with it? I know that your gnomes have a history with Greg and the boys and that's why I felt particularly bad about not getting right out there."

"They weren't at first," Debbie told her. "They were upset and confused, because who goes around taking things out of people's yards? But once they started seeing the posts, I think they all got a little excited about the gnomes' adventures. I honestly think we'll all miss it when it's done. As long as Hans gets back home safely," she added.

"We feel the same way," Brenda told her. "Here I thought I might have a hand in solving a big mystery, but I didn't. I showed up late to the party, I guess."

"Well, thank you for the update." Debbie meant the thanks sincerely. "It means a lot to all of us. I'm not sure how the Calloways feel about their leprechauns being the bad guys, but it's fun to see how NoPlaceLikeGnome can remake the background and insert them all into village scenes that either don't exist—"

"Like the forest that was really an unmown lot of weeds and brush," interrupted Brenda.

"Yes, exactly that. And the filled pots on Grant Street, the medieval flags. It's clear this person is good at the job."

"And at storytelling," noted Brenda. "Not everyone can weave a tale so well with just a few words and the angle of the shots. The expressions on their faces—and how guilty those leprechauns look when they get caught misbehaving."

"Which has been several days running."

"It sure has," agreed Brenda. "You have a good night," she added. "I'm sorry I didn't get out there in time and that I didn't catch a glimpse of how he got there or who took him away, but I won't deny that it might be fun to see the churchyard becoming part of the story."

Her words made Debbie smile. When she hung up the phone, she thought about calling Greg, but it was getting late. He had an early start in the morning on a job just outside New Philadelphia.

She'd fill him in tomorrow. For now, she puzzled on the thought of the towheaded gnome at the church gazebo.

Kelsey Addison's house was a five-minute walk from Faith Community. The Addisons lived right between Claymont Creek and the village church. Did that mean Kelsey was the phantom poster and illustrator?

No...

But if means, motive, and opportunity were the mainstays of solving a mystery, Julian's young friend still checked more boxes that anyone else on the suspect list.

CHAPTER THIRTEEN

Thursday morning saw customers streaming into the café for bakery orders, but the only visitors to the counter were Harry and Crosby and Jim Watson.

Paulette wasn't due in until seven thirty, so Debbie took care of the early morning customers while Janet baked and Charla frosted. Charla Whipple and her husband had run the Third Street Bakery for years. Janet had honed her baking skills by working for them until they retired and closed the bake shop. She'd brought those baking skills and recipes on board to the Whistle Stop Café. The amazingly delicious cakes, pies, cookies and muffins were a big part of Janet and Debbie's current success.

Debbie had propped the swinging door to make it easier for the others to access the pickup rack Janet had rolled in from the storage area. Jim Watson indicated the rack with a thrust of his chin as he took a seat alongside Harry. "You have all been up and at it, I see."

"You can always tell a holiday when the extra rack gets wheeled through the door. Charla and Janet are amazing together," Debbie said.

"Like they've done this before." Jim laughed and so did Harry.

"A well-oiled machine," Harry said. "Although no one makes breakfast like Debbie here. My doc is all over me because I indulge in those treats more than I should." He eyed the various bakery orders with a deliberately overdone sigh then winked. "But a couple of eggs over easy with some nice wheat toast would be just the thing this morning. And a scrambled egg for Crosby."

Crosby tipped his head up. When Debbie smiled down at him, the dog begged with his eyes. She laughed. "Your breakfast will be right along too, my friend. Who can resist those eyes?"

Harry patted the dog's head. "This fellow is a wonderful thing to wake up to," Harry assured them. "I know all's right and well when I wake up to Crosby looking for attention. He nudges that nose right up under my elbow and lets me know it's time to get up. Now, barking and dancing back and forth is another thing altogether." Harry's voice went deep. "He did that the other morning when that fellow was climbing down off the depot trains. Crosby was fit to be tied, but I told him to just leave it. Just someone doing maintenance for Kim, I told him, but he would have none of it until the fellow disappeared up the tracks near the old storage place."

Debbie had been about to pour Jim's coffee, but Harry's words made her pause. "Someone on the train cars, Harry? When was this?"

"Three or four days back," he told her. "He was at this end by the passenger cars, not up by the 2700."

The C&O 2700 had become a more recent addition to the depot museum, and the gleaming black steam engine had undergone a stunning renovation.

"I know Kim likes to keep things up properly." Harry stirred cream into his coffee as he spoke. "She doesn't like having a bunch of workers around during museum hours, so I figured someone needed to patch a leak or fix a seal and wanted it done early. Sun, wind, and snow can be tough on railroad cars."

Debbie wanted to press further, but it was obvious that Harry either wasn't aware of the gnome's online theatrics or hadn't put two and two together. At his advanced age, she didn't want to make him feel like he should have reported the sighting, although she'd like to know more about the man he saw. Just the fact that he saw someone was an interesting twist.

He might be right. It could have been someone working on the trains. A simple conversation with Kim would clear that up. But how interesting to have a fellow on the western end of the trains a couple of days before Hans staged a rooftop adventure heading east?

But if it wasn't a repairman, then was it Tucker? He was supposed to return on Monday, and the museum was closed on Mondays. He knew that. The café was open, but they were at the opposite end of the depot building and probably wouldn't have noticed something going on that far away.

If it was the person behind NoPlaceLikeGnome, that would mean he couldn't do everything with clever editing. He needed baseline shots to work from.

"It's always good to keep things up on these vintage pieces," Jim said. He said it to Harry, but he flashed Debbie a quick look of understanding.

"A stitch in time saves nine," Harry agreed. "My mama used that phrase, and it's something I've taken heed to all these years. Fix it quick and proper and you have less to worry about later on."

"Words of wisdom." Debbie slipped a rolled packet of silverware onto the counter for him. Then she filled a mug with coffee for Jim and set it in front of the newspaper editor. "Can I get you anything besides coffee this morning, Jim?"

He hesitated, then nodded. "Two scrambled eggs and rye toast would be nice. I was going to pass on breakfast, but I've got a few things to take care of later and then we've got the Maundy Thursday service at church tonight, so I'll have breakfast and lunch and won't worry about missing dinner."

"Sounds like a plan." She refilled Harry's coffee, then left the two men to chat. On her way to the grill, she motioned Janet aside.

Janet followed her to the far side of the kitchen. "What's up?"

Debbie repeated what Harry had said.

Janet winced. "Tucker and Dean Addison go way back. Dean's his godson, and he was a big help when Kelsey was in the hospital for so long."

Dean Addison's daughter had been diagnosed with leukemia as a small child. She'd been cured for years, but the illness had taken a toll on her family.

"They're still best friends," Janet continued. "So maybe Tucker is getting shots and Kelsey's editing them? Putting together the montage?"

"That creates the level of means we needed," whispered Debbie. "I know Kelsey's got the skills, but I couldn't see how she could be taking photographs or being in places to get photos while she's doing the yearbook, school, cheering for Julian's team, and whatever else a fourteen-year-old kid is doing in April."

"You're still okay with stopping to see Tucker this afternoon?"

She sure was. If for no other reason than to put the pieces together and make sure Hans would be returned. "A surprise visit. Yes. Once we've got the Saturday orders mostly done."

Paulette arrived a few minutes later. She and Debbie took care of customers and orders. She grinned when she saw the metal rack had been brought back to its occasional place of honor. "When the rack comes on board, it's a sure sign the ovens are working overtime," she noted as she stowed her purse beneath the counter. She put her train-decorated apron on with a snap and a smile. "And me along with them. Good morning, ladies!" She pointed to the rack with a nod of approval. "And thank you for organizing the baked goods by their pickup time and the name. Makes my job easier when people come in."

"Charla gets full credit for that," explained Janet. "Names are hard to categorize on busy days, but time slots never have to be re-sorted."

"I see that." Paulette handed over breakfast orders for two tables, then headed back to fill coffees and do silverware setups.

The café was busy from eight o'clock on. Greg came in for a coffee a little after nine. Harry was on his way out with Crosby. Greg held the door wide for him, wished him a good day, then crossed the floor. He leaned on the counter from one side.

Debbie did the same from her side. They both grinned. They didn't kiss, but they didn't have to. There was simply something wonderful about being in the same place at the same time.

Jim cleared his throat.

"Young love," Paulette said.

Jim laughed. "That's it all right."

Debbie smiled as she filled Greg's to-go mug. "It's quite nice, actually."

"I concur." Greg winked at her. "Are we meeting at church tonight, or are you coming over to the house after work?"

"Here's the plan." She handed him his coffee and ticked off her fingers. "We're finishing as much baking as we can, then we're stopping at Holmstead Gardens to see Tucker Lewis, then going home to get ready for the service. Since it starts at six thirty, I'll meet you guys at the church, okay?"

"Why Holmstead Gardens and why Tucker?" Greg asked.

Jim had gotten up. He crossed to the cash register while they talked. Debbie lowered her voice as she explained her earlier conversation with Harry. "Harry actually *saw* someone on one of the railcars," she told him. "If it's not someone who was hired to work on the cars, it could be our online poster. You know how Tucker loves to see the town get good press. Good notice. Maybe this clever campaign is his idea. We thought we'd ask."

"But why the garden store?" asked Greg. "Tucker and his dad run Lewis Concrete & Stone."

"LC&S is building a retaining wall for one of this year's garden displays," she answered. "He posts his schedule online so potential customers can see their worksites and check their results. If we stop in to see him at the garden center, I can look at annuals for the borders too."

"Which shouldn't be planted for a few weeks to avoid overnight frosts." He added the reminder with a knowing smile.

"Preparation is a big part of creativity and future success," she told him. She stretched up and kissed his cheek. "I'll see you at church tonight. Okay?"

"Yes, ma'am." Greg turned to Paulette. "Mom, do you want to ride with me and the boys tonight? Or would you rather walk?"

More customers had just come in, but Paulette stopped a moment before seating them. "I'll walk tonight. It'll give me a chance to ponder. There's no rain or snow in the forecast."

"Then we'll see you there."

Greg headed out.

A steady influx of customers made the day fly by. It was nearly four by the time they had the majority of cake, cookie, pie, and bread orders made, decorated, and packed.

"I know you two have someplace to be." Charla waved a green-and-white striped dishcloth in the air as Janet switched the ovens off. "I'll finish cleaning up. You head out. That way you won't be rushed for church tonight. My service doesn't start till later."

Her words were a time-saving relief. Debbie had been thinking they'd never have time to clean and close the café, make the drive, see Tucker, and get back in time to get ready for the service. "Thank you!"

"And I'm taking this pile of aprons home to wash," said Janet as she tossed a handful into a bag. "We can start tomorrow fresh."

New Philadelphia was fifteen minutes away. Debbie drove. Taking two cars would be silly, and this way she could run some things by Janet. "Can we do a wedding checklist on the way?"

"Sure can!" Janet had her notebook and pencil out before they'd pulled out of the depot parking area. "Church?"

That was an easy one. "Chosen!"

"Date?"

"Mulling."

Janet groaned but kept going. "Matron of Honor?"

Debbie laughed. So did Janet because there was never any doubt between the two of them of who would have that honor if and when either of them married. Debbie had served as Maid of Honor years ago for Janet and Ian's wedding. That pledge had never changed.

"Dress chosen!" Janet didn't have to ask about that one. She'd been part of that special evening. "And alterations begun?"

"That's an absolute positive," Debbie replied. The seamstress appointment had been wonderfully simple. "Almost done, in fact. It's the advantage of being on the taller side and choosing a fairly simple gown. That meant it only needed a hem and a little nip here and there."

"Wonderful." Janet made another check on the list. "Best men?"

"Also done. We got their suits last weekend. Who knew that it would be just as hard to shop for boys' suits?"

Janet commiserated as she made a note on the page. "Being married to a man has taught me they're not as simple as they may appear."

"That's 100 percent correct." Debbie took the turn north, toward New Philadelphia.

"Reception?"

"Site unsure, but Ricky at Buona Vita said he'd be happy to cater whatever we want."

"He did?" Janet paused then said, "Buona Vita doesn't do catering. How'd you score that deal?"

"His appreciation for our help when things went awry for them and years of business with my family," she replied. She paused for a vehicle making a left turn, then continued once they were on their way again. "He said he's always had a soft spot for love stories, and he's never forgotten how many times my parents and I sat in our favorite booth to celebrate milestones. Including my engagement to Reed and my coming back here to open the café with you. He said for this—" She smiled. "*For us*, he would make an exception. So now we just need a venue and a date."

Janet fist-pumped the air. "We're getting there! And once we have that we can do invitations, response cards, stamps, menu planning, cake ideas, linens, napkins, color schemes. You've gotten so much done, Debbie! That's wonderful!"

Janet's additions to the list made Debbie's stomach clench.

She wasn't an overly anxious or emotional person. She never had been, but hearing Janet's litany of things yet to be done—

"Oh, and flowers. And music." Janet's voice danced as she added those to her list.

Debbie didn't dare speak.

It wasn't that she didn't want to make decisions or plan. It just seemed like so much for one day. Yes, it was a very special day, but was it any more special than the day Greg proposed? That beautiful moment on Valentine's Day when they both knew they wanted to spend the rest of their lives together?

In her mind *that* was the big moment. The wedding was important, yes, but the trappings of the wedding didn't matter as much to her as they might to a younger bride.

Greg mattered. Julian and Jaxon mattered. Their life together mattered. But the rest was like whipped cream on a sundae. If you ran out of whipped cream, the sundae was still amazing, so if every detail of this wedding wasn't magazine perfect, maybe that was the better way. Maybe that's why she'd been avoiding some of these decisions.

"I'll talk to Greg this weekend," she told Janet. "We'll nail down details. I promised you and my mom that we'd have a firm plan in place by the end of the month, right?"

Janet tapped the notebook for effect. "And you're well on your way. So you talk to that handsome hunk of yours, and we'll go from there. Wow." She whistled softly as Debbie pulled into the generous parking lot of the beautiful garden store at the edge of New Philadelphia. "Isn't that something to see?"

Tucker Lewis and his crew were working on the far left. They had constructed a stunning water garden complete with tumbled stone, a waterfall, a retaining wall, multiple pump stations, and a double pond feature.

Debbie parked the car.

They climbed out and headed Tucker's way. It didn't take an expert to see that his work wasn't just lovely. It was intricate with a touch of forested beauty that showed through the tiny fairy homes and gardens half hidden in the burbling water setting.

That bit of fancy might be the giveaway when all was said and done, because their internet poster clearly had an eye for whimsy.

So did Tucker Lewis.

CHAPTER FOURTEEN

O
h my goodness. This is beautiful!" Janet exclaimed as they approached the water display.

"Stunning," agreed Debbie. "I'm not sure I can live without something like this in our backyard now. I'm gobsmacked."

"That kind of reaction makes all the work worth it." Tucker said. He'd been putting small stones into place. He wiped his hands on a cloth as he stood, then stuffed the rag back into his pocket. "Nice to see you ladies." He flashed them a quick smile. "Give me a moment, okay?"

"Of course."

They watched as he took multiple camera shots of the ongoing project. Once done, he stepped back. He gave one of the workers a thumbs-up, then came their way.

Debbie indicated the gorgeous landscaping with a low whistle. "This whole thing is amazing, Tucker. Is it your design?"

"Mine and Ralph's," he told them. "Ralph Whitaker. He graduated from Claymont with me and went on to apprentice with a stone guy in Kentucky about twenty years ago. He returned a few months ago and bought his parents' place in north Uhrichsville. He's got an eye, and a real good feel for the mix of stone and water and GPH." He must have seen Janet's frown. "Gallons per hour."

"Ah." Janet nodded understanding. "That makes sense."

"It's a direct relationship from the capacity of the pump or pumps to the stone's height and width and the water tumble. He's been a great asset to the team."

"That's wonderful. And the fairy houses and gardens? Are those a credit to him too?" Debbie asked. "Because they're adorable."

"That's actually me," he replied.

His admission made Debbie and Janet exchange a quick glance. "Me and Kelsey," he added.

"Oh?" Janet pretended a look of surprise toward Debbie, who recognized it right away. "They're super cute. Kind of whimsical."

"That describes Kelsey to a T," he went on. "Cecily wanted to put a water garden in their backyard, and Kelsey wanted to help her grandma. You know Cecily, right?" He redirected his attention to Debbie for a moment. "She lives just up the road from Greg's house."

"Yes, she's a very nice neighbor."

"Well, Kelsey loves doing things like this, and Cecily thought it would be fun to do it in the backyard near the patio. She likes the sound of trickling water. I built the feature and installed it, but Kelsey added the cutesy stuff. Like this." He indicated one of the "fairy" features, a hollowed log nestled onto a thick wood round. The log was surrounded by small silk flowers, a miniature swing, and a tiny fairy peeking out from the nearest open end. "The minute she did that, I realized what our designs were missing. I talked to Ralph and we decided to run with the idea. Kelsey does some of the work, but Ralph's got two daughters who love this stuff too. The three of them are working to create fairy houses and gardens to use in our landscaping designs. They're going to work over the summer to create stock for us. It's driven interest in the water features more than double last year's volume."

Janet reached down and touched the nearest fairy house. "It really brings the fanciful side of this to life, doesn't it?"

"Exactly," he said. "I never thought about injecting an element like this into our work until Kelsey came along with her ideas. Now we're hooked, and the girls will make extra money for college, if that's what they're looking to do in a few years."

"It's marvelous, Tucker. You know what it reminds me of?"

Debbie knew where Janet was leading. Tucker didn't, so she watched his reaction carefully and tried to look like she wasn't watching for his reaction at all.

"What's that?"

"The funny posts you've shared on the town's feeds. The gnomes and the leprechauns and the shenanigans going on."

"Those posts have driven our engagements up by several hundred percent," Tucker told her. He didn't even try to hide his excitement. He folded his arms and embraced the conversation twist with a look of satisfaction. "It's like clickbait. People click 'like' or 'love' or 'laughter' and the algorithms bring us into their feed more often. That benefits the village and every business in town that uses our page for information and promotion. We all benefit by additional discoverability. Who'd have thought that an innocent story about little statues would get so many people talking?"

"Well, we kind of saw that with the creepy doll in Texas, didn't we?" Janet met Tucker's gaze evenly. "I remember how you loved those posts."

"Keller, Texas." He clicked his tongue against the roof of his mouth. "I had no idea something so minor could go viral. The minute I saw it, I realized what wonderful potential it had. People from all over the world were checking out those little videos. It was unbelievable. Unbelievably good," he continued. "It's several years later, and people still go to their site to see the videos. That's staying power. I've racked my brain trying to come up with something to drive up our visitors, then this came along. Crazy, right?"

"Or strategically planned by a couple of people who work well together."

Tucker frowned. "I don't know. I—" He paused as Janet and Debbie exchanged looks, then his frown went deeper. "You think I could be doing this? Me, putting together the antics of those yard ornaments before sharing them on our town site?"

"Kelsey doesn't just have a great eye for whimsy," Janet reminded him. "She's skilled way beyond her years at graphic arts and design. We thought if you were providing the photographs—"

"And Kelsey was manipulating them with her computer software—" added Debbie.

"That maybe you two were working together to bring more notice to the town and the town's readership."

Tucker scrubbed a hand to his head. Then he whooshed out a breath. "I'd love to say it's my brainchild, but my brain doesn't work that way." His admission was tinged with regret. "I appreciate imagination and creativity. That's why Ralph and I jumped on the opportunity to have the girls make these fairy scenes once Kelsey added them to her grandmother's display. Once we added them in here, people's reactions were almost instantaneous. They like the majesty of the waterfall, but that isn't what's making them stop and grab a brochure or call us for an estimate. It's the chipmunk peeking out of the moss-covered stump there." He pointed to the water garden's upper edge. "Or the painted turtle on the far side. Or the five dragonflies Kelsey hung from fishing line."

The dragonflies were hung at varying heights, like they were hovering in a midsummer garden. Debbie had liked them straight off.

"The slightest breeze makes them move, but you have to look hard to see the clear line. Ralph and I think the fairy houses invite people to a simpler time. A simpler place. That's what they sign up to have us re-create for them, so business is booming. But that's it, ladies."

"Could it be someone else working with Kelsey?" Janet pressed. "But who else is so invested in having the town's accounts get noticed? And if it's not you, why would an eighth grader like Kelsey care? It's not like kids are flocking to the town's pages to see what's going on. Parents, yes. Kids, no."

He shrugged. "I'm over the moon to have people coming to the town's social media pages every day, but I'm not the kind of guy who can put that together. You're right though." He made a face, pondering. "Kelsey's got adult-level skills when it comes to that stuff, so maybe she is working with someone else. She told me that a few of her teachers match her up with others on a regular basis because she's a good team leader."

Debbie had seen the truth in that with Julian. "She's a natural leader, I agree. The English teacher paired her up with Julian and it was a big help. She helped him see the focus of the story. Well, Tucker." She sighed purposefully. "I was really hoping you were part of this. Although I'm not as upset as I was initially when our statue disappeared, because whoever is doing this seems willing to return things. Once he or she is done with them."

"Well, that's the other thing," Tucker told them. "Bud would have my head if I pilfered things out of people's yards, even if it helps the town in the end. You know how aboveboard he is."

Debbie couldn't disagree. She'd never heard or observed anything about the mayor that would indicate otherwise.

"You ladies are looking for someone with a broader scope for imagination than I have. I'd check with Amelia and Dean before approaching Kelsey," he advised. "See if it's okay to ask Kelsey about it. They're still a little protective of her after all she went through as a little kid, even though they both know she's doing fine. If Kelsey's involved, she'll say so. She's imaginative, but there's not a dishonest bone in her body. And I'm glad that whoever *is* responsible is returning things they borrow when they're done with them, right?"

Debbie nodded but added a caveat. "Borrowing is a loose term when you haven't asked permission."

"I hear you," Tucker said. "Bud was upset initially, thinking we had kids messing with people's stuff, especially after we've worked so hard to bring the village up to date and give it the ambiance Bud always wanted for it. He's proud of that record."

"So are we." Debbie touched the top of the Lewis Concrete & Stone sign nearby. "And we know you donated a lot of stone to make those new paths happen, Tucker. They're beautiful."

Her words made him smile. "My mom loved this town. She had so many stories about her grandparents and World War II. My grandpa and my uncles served. Four McClaren boys, all army. My grandpa came through the war, but only one of his brothers managed to make it home. He lost the other two. One in Europe and one in the Pacific. His younger brother, Thomas McClaren, was a POW at Palawan in the Philippines. He was killed while being held there. A few months later my Uncle Michael—the uncle that made it back home—was one of the Army Rangers that joined forces with the Filipinos to free the detainees at several camps after what happened at Palawan. Helping this town that helped so many others runs in our blood, on both sides of the family."

His phone rang.

Janet gave the phone a wave of acknowledgment. "You take care of that, and thank you for your thoughts. We'll give Dean and Amelia a visit."

He moved off.

Debbie glanced at her watch. "I was going to look at annuals, but I can do that over the next few weeks. Let's head home. We can chat on the way."

"Good idea." They went back to the car.

Janet was busy scribbling down notes as Debbie left the parking space. When she was done writing, she sighed. "So we know who *didn't* do it. Right?"

"Yes," Debbie agreed as she turned onto the street. "Pretty sure, anyway. Nothing he said was definitive proof, just a denial. But it was nice talking to him and getting his thoughts. My gut tells me we can cross him off the list."

"He did suggest someone else might be helping Kelsey. He didn't seem opposed to the idea of her involvement, so that brings us around to the guy on the train a few days ago."

"Let's ask Kim after services tonight," suggested Debbie as they headed toward Dennison. "That will wrap up that tidbit of information one way or the other."

And they would have done that, except that Kim Smith wasn't at church. When Debbie texted her to see if everything was fine after the service, Kim sent her a happy emoji. WENT TO SERVICES AT GOOD SHEPHERD WITH MOM AND RAY AND A BUNCH OF OTHERS, she texted back. WE'RE HAVING CAKE NOW. DO YOU NEED ME TO CALL?

Debbie didn't want to interrupt their gathering time. WE CAN TALK TOMORROW.

Kim sent back a thumbs-up emoji.

Greg and the boys had been talking to one of the baseball coaches in the vestibule. They all came out together. Debbie caught the tail end of the conversation as the coach addressed Jaxon.

"Your game has improved significantly." The assistant coach had to look up to Jaxon now, after the teenager's winter growth spurt. "If you keep this up, you'll be playing varsity next spring."

Anticipation brightened Jaxon's expression. Debbie wondered if the coach knew the impact of his words. How much they meant to a growing adolescent whose gangly arms and legs didn't behave exactly like they used to.

Greg shoulder-nudged him as the coach proceeded toward the parking lot. "Your work ethic is paying off."

Jaxon blushed.

Greg ignored the reaction and met Debbie's gaze as she came closer. "It's not every Holy Week that the ice cream stand is open, but with Easter being late this year it is. I say we go get a treat and take it home. The wind's picking up, but I could go for a hot fudge sundae right about now, and I bet I'm not the only one."

The boys raced to the truck, and Debbie breathed a sigh of relief when neither one fell or pushed the other out of the way.

Greg reached for her hand. He wrapped it in his and squeezed lightly. "I couldn't be happier, Debbie. I mean that. Totally."

She could have teased him about buttering her up so she'd pay for the ice cream, but she didn't.

Instead she simply leaned up for a quick kiss. "Me too. And honestly, Greg?" She paused and held his gaze with hers. "There is nothing else I need or want. You. The boys. A beautiful life right here, in this town. That's my dream come true."

He squeezed her hand lightly again and smiled. "And a hot fudge sundae."

She smiled back at him. "And that."

CHAPTER FIFTEEN

Easter weekend couldn't have been better.

The poignant Good Friday church services served as a reminder of God's pure love.

Janet and Ian were thrilled that Tiffany was able to come home for the weekend.

The weather cooperated fully. Tulips popped into bloom across the village, dressing up yards with bright and cheerful blossoms.

The café itself was quiet by Saturday afternoon. All the orders had been picked up in a timely manner, and the bakery case was pretty much empty.

"That's a welcome sight," noted Paulette as she removed the final offerings and packed them into a heavy-duty tote. "I'll take these to the food pantry on my way home. Oh, here's Kim, looking for that midday coffee, no doubt."

"And feeling way overdue," Kim replied. "It wasn't all that busy, so I assigned myself a bunch of catch-up tasks and pretty much bogged myself down." She turned to Janet and Debbie. "Sorry I couldn't make it in yesterday. Madison twisted an ankle in Thursday's soccer game, and they wanted her to rest on Friday. Her mom and dad were both working yesterday, and I knew I was covered here."

"How's she doing?" Debbie finished wiping the counters while Paulette washed the tables.

"Thankfully she's fine and we shouldn't have to worry, although I could tell she wasn't happy when the doctor told her to sit out this next week."

"Oh, they never like to hear that," agreed Debbie. "We had a quick question for you but didn't want to pester you with it while you were with your mom. Harry mentioned that he saw a man coming down from the top of one of the passenger cars several days back. He used the access ladder on the far side. Harry and Crosby could see him, but the trains would have blocked our views from here. Harry said it was early in the day, before opening. We wanted to know if you'd hired anyone to do work on top of the cars. We know you like to get maintenance done before the museum opens."

Kim offered them a blank expression as she shook her head. Then her face changed. She looked at all three women and folded her arms. "NoPlaceLikeGnome, right? Unless someone decided to climb up to the top of a train going nowhere, who else could it be? Did Harry recognize him?"

Debbie shook her head. "No. Crosby sounded the alarm like the good dog he is. When Harry went to his back window to see what the fuss was about, he saw a man climbing down from one of the passenger cars."

"What did he look like?" asked Kim.

Debbie shrugged. "Harry said he looked ordinary. Like anyone working outside would. Jeans. Gray hoodie, and the hood was up. We thought it might be Tucker Lewis," she added. "That maybe he was working on the promotion to give the town's social pages and businesses an extra push, but he wasn't. We wanted to touch base with you and see if you knew anything about it."

"Nothing at all," said Kim. The admission didn't seem to make her happy. "The thought of someone climbing up there and playing around doesn't sit well. I'm glad whoever it was didn't fall or get hurt."

"The photographer seems to know what he's doing," Debbie said. "Certainly the poster's good at photo editing, but it would help if you have a good shot to start with. He'd need a certain perspective at different times of day to present his stories. Wouldn't he?"

"Of course." Kim nodded. "You'd want the right perspective so you could manipulate the photos. I'm not good at it," she told them, "but my friend's niece does graphic design for a big marketing firm in Atlanta. It's amazing what you can make things do now, and how you can make them look."

Janet layered a thick swirl of whipped cream onto Kim's coffee, then added a caramel drizzle. "That will get you through till Monday."

"I'll see if I can get any good camera footage of this guy. The cameras don't catch the far side of the railcars, so if he was careful, we might not get much or anything at all. But if he didn't realize that, or turned to look at the depot, maybe we'll get lucky. Are you two ladies okay with waiting until I come in on Tuesday? Or would you like me to pop over on Monday and check out the recordings?"

"Tuesday's fine," Debbie assured her. "But if you're not busy, Monday would be better."

That made Kim laugh. "Monday it is. I admit to being more than a little enthralled by this storyline myself. How anyone can take random yard ornaments and turn them into a rather brilliant story amazes me. It's like we're watching a book being written before our eyes and we get to see the work in progress. I'll come by on Monday."

"Great."

"I get until tomorrow evening at five o'clock to enjoy having Tiffany home," added Janet. "I'm going to soak it up. It's not like this guy is doing any harm. He might even be doing more good than harm at this point. But without permission."

Debbie's phone signified a text. She read it, then slipped the phone into her pocket. "Well, Greg just installed two out-of-sight cameras in the front yard and two on the house. When whoever this is returns our now romantically involved gnome couple, we'll get him—"

"Or her," interjected Janet, and Debbie agreed.

"Yes, if there are two of them working, we'll see them. I know these days security teams recommend cameras," she added as she turned toward the kitchen. They had a small amount of cleanup still to do, and it was time to get to it. "But I hate that it has to be that way in our hometown. Are you seeing your mom tomorrow?" she asked Kim. Kim's mother had stepped in as the depot's stationmaster during World War II. She'd been instrumental in turning a casual rail stop into a depot that became a fond memory for hundreds of thousands of troops that rolled through on their way to deployment. Over four thousand volunteers worked tirelessly for years to make sure every military man or woman knew they were appreciated and that a country of patriots stood firmly behind them.

Kim breathed in the scent of her coffee and smiled. "I'm spending Easter with Mom at Good Shepherd. The morning, anyway. Then we're having dinner at my nephew's just outside of town. Happy Easter, ladies!"

"Same to you." Janet called the words as she hurried to clean up the coffee area.

Debbie did the same to the one corner of the kitchen that still needed a wipe-down.

As the three women moved to the door a few minutes later, Debbie's phone buzzed.

So did Janet's.

Debbie swiped her phone open and there was Hans, dressed in a miniature suit and tie, walking up to an equally dressed-up Greta. *Except that Greta is home. In the garden. Isn't she?*

The picture presented a perfect angle of the little couple. Hans, moving forward, looking deliriously happy and smitten, which was a far cry from the gnome's normally placid expression. Greta, looking like a young bride, sweet and flirtatious. In everyday life, the Dutch statue sported an enigmatic Mona Lisa countenance. Barely there, a whisper of contentment.

Not today.

Lashes down—lashes that didn't exist on the real Greta—she peeked up at the approaching Hans and rewarded him with a lovely smile.

"That's amazing." Debbie stared at the pics and sighed. "How he can turn these two simple statues into something out of a storybook is beyond me. I mean the gnomes are cute, but this"—she indicated their adorable expressions with a look of appreciation—"this is amazing. And the apple blossom background makes the whole picture sing with love."

"'In the spring a young man's fancy lightly turns to thoughts of love.'" Paulette shoulder-nudged Debbie with the Tennyson quote as they moved toward the café door. "Remind you of anyone? My son, perhaps?"

It did, actually. The whole charming scene, rimmed with the pink-and-white of fresh apple blossoms. "It does. But did they come and steal poor little Greta? Again?"

Janet looked chagrined. "Maybe?"

Paulette called Greg, and when he answered, she put him on speaker. "Can you run outside and see if Greta is still there? In the garden? Because someone just posted—"

"Sure. Hang on. I'll head that way right now." A moment of silence ensued, and then they heard Greg sigh. "Nope. Gone. I'd say I was pretty sure she was there this morning, but to be honest, I didn't check. I installed the cameras without even checking on her because I was focused on the task at hand. Sorry."

A few weeks ago Debbie hadn't been just irked about the statue's disappearance. She'd been angry. Now she was—

"Wait." Greg's voice interrupted her thoughts. His tone held a sense of urgency. "There's a note."

"A note?" The three women exchanged looks, and Debbie paused, waiting to hear what the note said.

"It says, 'Home soon. I promise.'"

Debbie drew back and looked at Janet, then Paulette, then Janet again. "That's it?"

"That's it."

Debbie took a few seconds to think it through, then aimed for the car once they were outside. "Whoever this is, he's good," she told Greg. "Or they're good. It is cute to see our very own gnomes cavorting in a delightful and unexpected romance, but I don't have time for this now. It's Easter weekend, and there's a real live family to take care of, so I'm going to come home and color eggs with you guys. Then Julian's going to help me make Easter bread."

The old-fashioned European bread was a recipe Debbie's mother always made, a braided loaf she glazed with spreadable icing. Before the icing dried, her mother would decorate half of the bread with tinted coconut. Not everyone was a fan of coconut, and Mom liked making people happy.

"Home soon," she added. It wasn't technically her home yet. But it would be soon.

"Looking forward to it."

She was too.

Still, her thoughts returned to NoPlaceLikeGnome. Whoever was "borrowing" items from people's yards and cleverly returning them had a distinct talent.

Good for him. Or her.

But whoever this was, taking their statues repeatedly without permission was gutsy and bold. That only made her more determined to figure out his or her true identity.

But not tonight.

CHAPTER SIXTEEN

*D*ebbie breathed in brisk, clean air at seven fifteen on Easter morning.

It felt wonderful. Absolutely, positively wonderful. She hugged Greg's arm as they walked around the open-air courtyard behind the church. The old-fashioned rectory was to their left, and its gleaming white porch was surrounded by an array of gorgeous spring flowers, which carried over into the square linking the rectory to the church. She breathed deeply again as they moved toward the gathering space now that the sunrise service was over. "Look how shiny and perfect everything is. It almost glows."

The birds didn't mind the early morning chill. They darted from tree to tree, stopping by a couple of feeders on the way, singing sweet songs of spring. As the mid-April sun stretched higher, each blade and petal glistened like a sugar-dusted cookie in a well-lit bakery case.

Greg swept the pretty churchyard a look of appreciation. "Everything shimmers on a morning like this."

They exchanged smiles.

It was easy to do when the day and the prayers and the service were all so beautiful.

"Is it okay if we go ahead to get doughnuts?" Julian posed the question, but Debbie was pretty sure Jaxon put him up to it.

"Yes, of course. But see if any of the older people need help, first. Okay?"

"Got it!" The boys hurried ahead to the promise of fresh dough-nuts from Glazed, the doughnut shop that had opened where the Third Street Bakery used to be. The crew there made great dough-nuts, and today's sampling was stellar. They'd boxed up an array of vanilla cream-filled, chocolate-filled, crullers, fried cakes, and lemon-filled and frosted. They included a separate big box of their famous maple-and-bacon doughnuts, a new favorite around town. Juice and coffee rounded out the doughnut tables.

She and Greg went inside for the fellowship—mostly. But a maple-and-bacon doughnut soon called her name. She decided to enjoy the pastry guilt-free, but a woman paying for dress alterations didn't want to go too far. She refused to worry about it today, though. Today was a day of celebration. New life. New love.

Pastor Nick came their way, smiling. "I'm glad you were able to come," he said. "We didn't have a big crowd, but a nice one. And enthusiastic." He included everyone near with a joyful gesture. "We've got a lovely day in store for all of us. He is risen!"

He said it loud enough for others to hear, and they responded with similar smiles. "He is risen, indeed!"

Greg took her hand as they moved through the door a half hour later. They'd decided to walk to church this morning. It had seemed like a risky decision at five forty-five when the thermometer was barely breaking forty, but the warming sun made Debbie feel almost overdressed now.

"I'm glad that we came to the sunrise service," Debbie said. She smiled. "And I think the boys are excited to have the day to themselves now. In fact, I heard Kelsey's coming over to finish up the last part of a project with Julian before dinner."

"Homework on Easter? That's news to me. But fine, of course." He eyed her. "Which means she may be setting herself up to be grilled about the gnome posts," he said dryly.

"Not grilled," she corrected him. "But..." She smiled and dragged out the word intentionally. "If it happens to come up in conversation, I may study her reaction. I've gotten over being upset," she admitted. Easter was a pretty good time to toss anger aside. "Now that I realize that the poster seems to mean no harm. Whoever it is has me wrapped up in the story too. Most of the town is loving this whole thing. Even the people whose gnomes disappeared a week back have gotten on board."

"Really?" Greg frowned. "They seemed very upset in the comments, and Ian said that Silas Thumm was fighting mad at first."

"Calmer heads are prevailing now because those two gnomes were dropped off at the thrift shop yesterday morning, before sunrise. Although a somewhat worn Home Sweet Home sign was taken from the bin, according to Margie. Maybe our miscreant decided a trade-off was in order?"

"Well at least we know that Tucker and Ian's idea about offering a neutral, no-questions-asked drop-off site worked."

"At least for those two gnomes. They're safely back in their own yard now."

"It amazes me that people have gotten so invested in the whole thing," Greg said. "I mean, it's cute. And engaging. It's certainly bringing in comments and reactions from way beyond our village borders," he continued. "But I wouldn't have predicted this. Ever. It's like we're all caught up in a kid's book and waiting for the next chapter to drop."

"You know your mother said that magazines used to publish stories this way when she was a child."

Greg lifted one eyebrow. "As in?"

"Serials. One chapter a month. You'd wait all month for the new edition to be delivered so you could see what happened next. I don't know if that would wash today," she added. "Books, yes. I love it when my monthly book order arrives. But single chapters drawn out to the next month? I don't know if that would work."

"With binge-watching happening all around us? I'd be afraid of a protest, but they did the same thing in one of the magazines Mom ordered for me when I was a kid, and I thought it was perfectly normal. That was thirty-five years ago. Either a whole different age or a blink of the eye, depending on perspective," he said. "A lot's changed since then."

"It has," Debbie agreed. "But whoever is doing this handles the storyline with an endearing humor and warmth. That helps me overlook the unconventional methods. It's like they've done this before. And using so many town settings is brilliant," she added. "That wins people over. The depot, the trains, the park, Grant Street. The new bike racks and the benches. The whole thing has turned out to be an advertisement for all the things that Bud and Tucker and the town council have been doing to update the village. People are loving it, and I expect we're going to see the rise in tourism they've wanted to inspire. Maybe even that filming contract that Bud was hoping for. I'd put Dennison, Ohio, up against any of the inspirational movie settings out there. Our little village has totally come into its own."

They'd reached the house. The boys had long since dashed on ahead.

She'd half wished that Hans and Greta would be returned for Easter. It was a silly wish. They were just statues. But she'd had this weird idea that having them home for Easter would make everything right.

Jaxon raced out of the back door just then with a basketball in his hand. Julian followed. They'd gotten changed, and a little one-on-one would get rid of whatever extra energy they'd stored up by sitting for an hour.

Seeing them getting along, laughing and talking as they banked and shot, reality hit her. They were all there. She and Greg, the boys, and soon the parents would arrive. In the end, that's what mattered.

Paulette was making the Easter ham. Debbie's mother was making her delicious scalloped potatoes, a crowd-pleasing favorite. Debbie had prepared a shrimp tray and salad. Dessert would be Janet's amazing tiramisu, a treat she only made for special orders and during the Christmas and Easter holiday seasons.

They had a lovely midafternoon dinner. The gentle weather and bright sun tempted them outdoors. A group of area kids had put together a touch football game in the vacant lot across the road. Greg had claimed the position of all-time-quarterback for both teams, and the eleven kids were having a great time. Her father had gotten one of Greg's coaching whistles and looked like he was having the time of his life as he mock-officiated the game.

Her father's joy was a wonderful example of how Debbie's new circumstances opened new roles of soon-to-be father-in-law and grandpa for him. His antics during the game affirmed that the retired assisted living manager was ready to embrace his new life wholeheartedly.

Dean Addison pulled into the driveway a little after four to drop off Kelsey.

Debbie had been chatting with Paulette and her mom. She spotted the car coming down the road and crossed to the driveway. Dean couldn't pull in far because of the number of cars, so she met him halfway up the slope. "Happy Easter, guys!"

Dean motioned toward the football game as Kelsey climbed out through the passenger door. "Think they'd mind if I popped in?"

"I think they'd love it. But first, can I ask Kelsey a question? About NoPlaceLikeGnome?"

"That little running comic strip has been the talk of our house for weeks," Dean told her as he exited the car. "Talk away. I'm going to see if I can get in on a few plays with the guys."

Kelsey came around the side of the car. She'd slung a small backpack over her shoulder. "My dad's not wrong. I love whatever that guy's doing. Or woman," she amended. "I want to be that good when I get older. It's funny, Mrs. Francis asked me at school if I was the one posting things, and I just laughed."

"You are good." Debbie kept it simple, because if others were noticing, she and Janet weren't too far off the mark.

Kelsey beamed. "Thank you! But you have to have an artist's skills to overlay so many things, flatten them, then bring up things almost out of nowhere to make the whole picture. When I look at NoPlaceLikeGnome's stuff, I can see exactly where my skills would leave off and his or her skills kick it up a notch. It would be awesome to meet the person behind it someday. They've taken graphic design and cartooning to a book-type level. It's a lot like the graphic novels we used to read in third and fourth grade. The Fisher twins. B.B. Baldwin made reading so much fun. Those books inspired me to want to take pictures and play with design. Some people say it's weird for a kid to like stuff like that."

"I don't think it's weird." Julian had left the game and crossed over to their side of the quiet street. "I think it's cool that you're so smart."

Kelsey blushed.

Julian didn't seem to notice, but Debbie did.

"Come on, let's get this over with, okay? Then we can go back to the football game if you want. If there's time."

"Yeah. Absolutely."

They hurried into the house. Finishing up their assignment shouldn't take them long, but their impromptu conversation with Kelsey had checked a few important boxes for Debbie.

She wasn't NoPlaceLikeGnome. Or at least, like Tucker, she said she wasn't, and Debbie had no reason to doubt her word.

If the online storyteller wasn't Tucker or Kelsey, who else had the skills and time to do something like this?

She had no idea. She called Janet ninety minutes later and repeated her conversation with Kelsey.

"Well, baseball mom, looks like we struck out." Janet sounded bemused. "I'm kind of at a loss. Kelsey said that her skills were weak by comparison?"

"Basically. Which means we're dealing with a pro. Advertising, maybe? Someone that has to create layered graphics for a job?"

"Not too many advertising agencies in Dennison."

Debbie knew that. "I'm clutching at straws. Let's shift topics. How was Easter with Tiff and your parents?"

"Wonderful. Ian got called away for an ambulance escort midday, but it wasn't anything super serious. He never complained a bit. Just said 'Back in a few.' It's amazing how long mashed potatoes can stay warm in a slow cooker," she said. "Thanks for talking to Kelsey when you got the chance. We may not have moved forward, but at least we can check her off the list."

"We can. She was quite convincing. I admit I was kind of surprised that we didn't get an Easter post about our gnome friends."

"Maybe our artistic borrower-then-returner is too busy with faith and family?"

"Most likely. Hey, I have a troop of guys heading my way for iced drinks and ham sandwiches."

"Didn't you just have dinner? Like three hours ago?"

Debbie laughed. "You forget how teenagers can eat. If dinner is at two, sandwiches are at five. Which means we're almost an hour past. See you tomorrow."

"Will do."

Originally she'd been amazed by the amount of food Greg and the boys could consume in a day, but she'd grown accustomed to it now. In a few short years, the boys would be off to school or work.

If having a full house meant some over-the-top grocery bills, she and Greg were fine with that.

CHAPTER SEVENTEEN

"I thought this day would never end." Janet sighed as they drove north toward Sugarcreek and the Bontrager store once they'd closed up the café the next afternoon. "After the busyness of last week, today was an absolute snoozer."

"With Paulette on board, it wasn't like we needed to do spring cleaning," agreed Debbie as she drove. "She keeps things in pristine shape every day, but it *was* a good day to clean the coolers. They sparkle now. If it was going to rain and be dreary, I'm glad it waited until today," she added with an eye to the dismal gray sky.

Janet scrolled her phone in the passenger seat. She paused and looked over at Debbie. "Do we have time to hit the Bontragers and stop by Bernice's house today?"

Debbie shook her head. "Baseball. Another makeup game."

"In the rain?" asked Janet, and Debbie nodded.

"It's just misty, so Jaxon's game is still on. And my dress is done, so I need to pick it up on our way back through New Philadelphia if you don't mind."

"Are you kidding? Something else to check off the list! Yes!"

"You can check off getting the license too," Debbie said as they drove the winding road up to Sugarcreek. "We got that done last week when the courthouse was quiet. It's good for a while, so we figured why not run in and take care of it? So we did."

"Well done." Janet added another check to her little pad of paper. "When's Jaxon's game, though? Won't we be messing that up?"

"No. It's a late game," Debbie explained. "They don't start until six forty-five. They're letting them play under the lights at the varsity field. It's meant to give them experience because the varsity team usually plays later in the day. Depending on how fast the game goes, they might only need the lights for the last inning or two. They sent out a text that they're not canceling for mist. Only if it really starts raining, because that would ruin field conditions. What about making a quick run to Bernice's place tomorrow?" she suggested. "The boys don't have any games, and I bet Paulette would be glad to pick them up for us if I get bogged down. Bernice's place is only ten minutes from the café."

Janet didn't seem to need convincing. "We can tell her we're checking on the cat."

"Which is true…" Debbie paused before she finished the thought. "In part."

"While also checking on what she's doing with all that lawn and garden stuff. I can't believe she's part of this online thing *intentionally*, but what if someone is using her collection habits for their own purposes? Taking advantage of her?"

"Is it taking advantage if it's not hurting anything?" Debbie weighed the thought carefully. "I guess that would depend on the circumstances, wouldn't it?" She mulled the question as they paused at a traffic light near the edge of town. "I was annoyed at first. Then puzzled. Now I'm puzzled and intrigued. I do hate having anyone consistently one step ahead of me." She angled Janet a frank look as they waited for the light to turn green.

"A quality that hasn't changed in forty years." Janet made the observation with a laugh, and Debbie couldn't disagree. She laughed along with Janet because they both knew it was true.

She pulled into the parking lot at Bontrager's fifteen minutes later. There were several vehicles parked alongside the building and three more parked out back, near the Bontrager home, including the gray car. The dank weather didn't seem to have a terrible effect on people seeking out quality goods from a skilled craftsman. Even with the mist, there were a few people milling around the outdoor swings, chairs, and shed exhibits.

"He does such nice work." Debbie motioned toward the sweetheart swings in the yard display behind the nicely appointed storefront. "Do you mind if we get a little wet?"

Janet popped up the hood on her café-themed sweatshirt. "No, ma'am."

Debbie did the same on her hooded jacket. They moved to the outdoor display area.

It was a warm day, and warm, rainy days in spring were wonderful for making the grass green and bringing lots of lonely earthworms to the surface. Today was no different. Earthworms of all sizes sought whatever earthworms seek by crawling across the paved driveway adjacent to the shop. The outdoor displays were done on gravel. None of the earthworms went that way. Clearly gravel wasn't a favored option.

"My mom calls this a worm rain," Janet said as she avoided the squiggly creatures.

"They are clearly unaware of the dangerous elements of car tires or wagon wheels," said Debbie. "And my mom calls it worm rain too. Because it smells funny."

"Yup. Earthworm funny."

Debbie spotted the swing she had in mind and pointed to it. "That's the one I'm after. We're after," she corrected herself. She gave Janet a wry look. "I have to remind myself to think and speak in the plural when I'm supposed to. Old habits die hard." She walked around the beautifully detailed swing and sighed. "Isn't it perfect? I love how Ephraim didn't go with the same design you see at so many shops. These inlaid hearts are perfect for us. I saw it last year when I was here shopping for gifts and I fell in love with it. It's quaint, charming, rugged, and ridiculously romantic, all at the same time." She drew out her phone and texted Greg a picture of the swing to make sure he liked it too.

"And yet you're not shopping for it together." Janet rolled her eyes. "I don't know if a romantic swing should begin with unromantic timing."

Debbie wasn't about to be dissuaded. "It should when you throw two kids, two jobs, two houses, and a dog into the mix." She smiled at Greg's affirmative text before bringing her attention back to Janet. "We've determined that shopping independently once in a while will give us more time to spend on the swing together."

Janet offered her a nudge of admiration. "Wise words."

"I might be new to this almost married-with-children scenario, but I'm learning." Debbie noted the price tag and motioned inside. "Let's get this paid for. I like the other ones, but this is exactly what I had in mind when Greg and I talked about it. Something we can use for three seasons of the year but all the seasons of life."

"Now that's romantic."

"Greg's words. Not mine. And yes, I do love it when he gets romantic." She exchanged a knowing smile with Janet as they walked to the gift shop door. "He's wonderfully sincere, and that's just another thing to love about him."

They went inside. Rhonda spotted them right off. She started to come their way, then stopped, like she was suddenly nervous, which was odd because when Debbie glanced around, she saw nothing to be nervous about.

She kept moving forward while Janet paused to look at some garden-friendly metal sculptures. Debbie stuck out her hand. "Debbie Albright from the café."

"Of course I remember. You came up to pick out your swing, perhaps?"

"I did," she replied. "I'd like to pay for it while I'm here, if that's all right. Greg's doing a job in New Philadelphia on Wednesday. He could swing up this way and pick it up when he's done. That saves me worrying that it might be gone by then because it's the last one of that kind out there."

"It *is* the last one until Ephraim is ready to do those more intricate cuts that the hearts require, so that is a smart move on your part. We started April with three of those, and now we are down to that one. I am glad you got here in time to see the full selection."

Janet had finished perusing the metal sculpture display. She came their way with her purse on one arm and a brightly painted metal rooster in the other.

Rhonda offered a smile. "You have found a friend, I see."

"I can't resist," Janet told her. "All this cuteness going on with the online story about gnomes and garden sculptures and flowers has me realizing I want to have a little more fun with my gardens than I've had in the past. That means this rooster goes home with me. I was thinking some of those bright wooden flowers too, Rhonda. My neighbor bought some earlier this month, and they add a nice splash of color to the borders."

"Like these?" Rhonda indicated a shelf full of multicolored tulips, but Janet shook her head.

"Not tulips, but thank you. I'm after the all-season ones. The neighbor has several yellow ones to liven up some drab bushes, and that's what I'm after. I've seen them around in all kinds of bright colors. Red, yellow, green, and orange with dark green leaves."

Rhonda pressed her lips into a thin line, then relaxed them. "I do know what you mean. They have been very popular the last few weeks."

Her words offered Debbie a light-bulb moment. "I wonder if that's because whoever's been posting the little stories about the town and the gnomes is using them in his or her posts?"

Rhonda pointed to a corner area that was nearly empty. "That's where they usually are, at least until the weather is dependable enough to do an outdoor display under the tent. We are totally out of them right now, although we've got more in the works. We whole-sale a number of things, including those wooden flowers, to Cassidy Clark. She does festivals all over southeastern Ohio. She figured they'd sell like hotcakes because of that story you speak of."

"She mentioned it when she came in?"

"Ja, and grabbed every one we had in stock to sell at the festivals. A hot item, she called them."

"Have you seen the story online?" asked Janet.

Rhonda shook her head. "I do not go online much. We try to limit things that pull our attention away from each other or our community. Part of our promise to God is to be fully present to our families, our neighbors, and our friends. I was happy to sell them to her," she continued. "But it will take a while to get more made. A week or more. Each flower requires three coats of paint, front and back. They do not dry quickly in this damp weather."

"Do you normally sell a lot of those flowers here too?" asked Debbie.

Rhonda nodded. "We sell a great deal of them. Their bright tones and reasonable price make them attractive to the tourists. They have also become popular among homeowners around Sugarcreek and down your way. The wholesale market has climbed the past few years, so we probably sell as many or more to vendors. The smaller garden add-ons have become a steady source of income for us."

"Are they difficult to make?" Debbie asked.

"That is another good thing about them. They are not hard to make even for someone with basic skills operating the saw. That has helped keep Benjamin busy while he is here. I paint them once the wood is dry enough to take it well. They last for years without chipping or peeling. Between the surgery and then the infection, Ephraim was not able to make the number he normally does. Having Ben here is a wonderful help to us. He is skilled enough to do easy things like that."

"Family can be a huge blessing at a time like this." Debbie turned to Janet. "I met Ben briefly in the pharmacy last week. He was worried that Ephraim was getting tired."

"And he was correct." Rhonda folded her arms lightly. "Ben is different from many in my family. He is my Englisch nephew," she explained. "That is fine with some in the family and not with others." She shrugged and sighed. "My brother Samuel and his wife moved to Philadelphia over thirty years ago. Samuel was the first one of our family to go to college, and that created a stir. We Mennonites were still part of the 'education stops at eighth grade' mindset then. Samuel was different."

Rhonda began straightening a display as she spoke. "We knew that, but his choices affected all of us. It created a chasm between some. For others..." Her expression grew more thoughtful. "It was more like a wall. There was a lot of squawking if you broke from the church." Debbie heard the sadness in her voice. "Loose lips. Angry words. But Samuel needed to be who God created him to be, and he and his wife Laurie have three great kids. They are grown now. Ben is the oldest. Such a smart, talented man. So creative."

"You sound proud of him," Janet said.

"I am pleased with the man he has become. When he heard Ephraim was having trouble, he came straight off because he works from home. He helped out over summers through college, and he learned how to do things quickly. He was born with a talent in his hands. Not everyone takes to creative woodworking. Although in Ephraim's family, I think it is in the blood."

"How nice that he has the time," noted Janet. "Sometimes that's the hardest part of helping. Managing a job and everything else."

"And that is part of the blessing," Rhonda went on. "He is able to do his work while he is here. I cannot pretend I know how it is done or even what is done, but it has been a good thing. He has cut out many flowers and leaves, gets his work done and keeps Ephraim's mind busy. Just having him here has been a godsend. He has taken Ephraim back and forth to physical therapy three times a week. That allows me time to mind the store."

"Is that why you were in Dennison last week?" asked Debbie, and Rhonda nodded.

"The therapy office has two locations, and I wanted to meet the people on his team—and make sure he was not being too grumpy with the workers." She sighed. "He is a good man, but he is not a fan of being laid up."

"No one is," Debbie agreed. "So we'll wait on the flowers, but I'll pay for the swing now. My compliments to Ephraim, the way he cut out those hearts. They're perfect."

Rhonda led the way back to the cash register. "He cares. If it does not come out right, he puts it in the cast-off pile to become a Christmas ornament or a tabletop item. But when it is my Ephraim at the saw, it is rare that they do not come out exactly like they should. And that is a fact."

They settled up for the swing and the rooster. It was still misty when they got to the parking lot. The mist, the trees, and the leaden clouds left everything a rather sodden gray, with deeper shadows along the edges and beneath the trees. "You'd never know it was nearly the end of April," said Debbie.

"And that it won't get dark for almost three more hours." Janet glanced up at the dense cloud layer above them. "One ray of sunshine would change all that."

Debbie was about to get into the car when she noticed an older man walking between the house and the broad display area adjacent to the wood shop. His gait was uneven, so she drew Janet's attention in that direction. "Is that Ephraim back there?" She jutted her chin toward the Bontragers' house. The other customers had left, with one exception, and that one was inside the shop with Rhonda.

Janet turned. "Sure is. That must be the nephew walking with him."

"It is. Yes."

Debbie watched them for a moment.

The older man's steps were awkward and uncertain. Despite that, the younger man seemed comfortable moving at the abbreviated pace.

He was talking.

Debbie couldn't hear what was being said, but the way his mouth and hands moved, it was clear he was on some kind of attention-grabbing topic. He gestured as he spoke, and a broad smile softened his face.

Debbie got in the car but didn't start it right away. She paused for a moment, then turned to Janet. "I see things differently now." She glanced beyond Janet, to the two men, walking as if it were a lovely day when it wasn't. "Different from how I saw them in Cleveland. Not the geography. Or even the population." She indicated the Bontragers' shop, then the two men walking along the farthest displays. "The family connections. How things work, how people work together, how they stand for one another. It's special. I missed that by being so far away."

"It can be." Janet had never been one to sugarcoat things. That was part of the reason they'd been friends for so long. They could be honest with one another, even when it was hard. "But you heard Rhonda in there. Sometimes a small town doesn't leave a lot of space for breathing room, and you just have to hang on through the tough times. I think that's what makes families like Rhonda's so special. They hung on even through the family rifts."

"And that's an element I was missing in my life." Debbie gave the men one last look as she started the engine. "It wasn't until the last few years I was there that I realized it. I'm not saying my life was empty," she added as she backed out of the spot. "It just wasn't as full as I wanted it to be. Maybe as I expected it would be." She turned into the southbound lane. "I don't know if it was facing that fortieth birthday or a midlife crisis. Maybe it doesn't even have a name, and that's okay too. Coming back home, opening a business with you, and living this new life has made me happier than I ever dreamed of being a few years ago. And that wasn't just me making that decision, Janet." She took a deep breath. "That was God nudging me."

"One of those Holy Spirit moments," agreed Janet. She smiled as she said it, and Debbie returned the smile.

"Yes. I am so glad I took Him up on the offer. Even though I was pretty sure we might crash and burn. I've never run a business like this before."

"And if we had?"

"We'd have dug in our heels and started all over again. It's not the falling down that gets us."

Janet agreed. "It's the failing to get back up." They rode in thoughtful silence for a while before Janet spoke again. "So we're good to swing out to Bernice's place tomorrow for a quick visit? And maybe a glance around?"

"Yes. Although it doesn't make a whole lot of sense, does it? The likelihood of Bernice being part of something like this is small. Yet the physical evidence says otherwise."

"So we follow the trails—"

"Even the bad ones."

Janet acknowledged that with a nod. "Because you never know where the puzzle piece might be hiding. Buried in Bernice's garage?"

"Or in plain sight. But there haven't been too many of those with this puzzle, have there? Except the perpetrator does return things. Then takes them again."

Janet frowned. "Not exactly normal thieving behavior, is it?"

"That's just it." Debbie hit her blinker to take the turn to Dennison. "Nothing about this is normal. There's no end game, is there? Or do we just not see it?"

Janet seemed just as puzzled. "It's a different score card. I'm not sure how to tally the points. Whoever is doing this is having fun with it."

"Loads."

"And causing no harm. Yet, it irks me that he or she is fooling us and we haven't been able to figure it out. It seems like this case should be even *more* obvious than others because the person has to have been all over town taking pictures and snatching lawn ornaments. How have they not been seen or captured on camera? Other than the railcar possibility, we've got no visual. On top of that, the only person who stands to gain is the village, and the village isn't a person. It's an entity. So why do it? Because this person loves Dennison?"

"Which circles us back to Tucker, but we believed him when he said it was way above his skill set." Debbie took one more turn toward Janet's house. "He's loving it, but I don't think he's got anything to do with it. I think he'd confess the minute we asked the question."

"What if we're on the wrong track, then?" Janet drummed her fingers on the dashboard.

Debbie pulled into Janet's driveway and put the car into park, then turned to face her friend.

"What if it started with targeting you, then grew out of proportion and the person either couldn't or wouldn't stop when they started having fun with all the attention?" Janet suggested.

That thought didn't add up for Debbie. "So that's Kelsey trying to show her grandmother that yard decor has its own place in the hearts of the people?" She sat up straighter as a thought occurred to her, one she hadn't considered till just now.

"What are you thinking?" Janet asked.

"Well, we've forgotten about Alicia. Could she have snitched the gnomes that belonged to Holly, her best friend, fearing I might get rid of them? Or for sentimental value? But then, if Alicia took the statue because she's upset about me marrying Greg, she certainly wouldn't be so playful about it. Would she?"

Janet shook her head. "I wouldn't think so. But we do know that Kelsey was only a few minutes away from the last photo shoot we know of, at the church, and that Brenda saw Hans there. Only a kid would assume they could get away with that in broad daylight."

"Or a kid at heart."

"And there's no one like that on our list."

Debbie frowned, but the frown disappeared quickly when Greg called a moment later. His voice came through the car's speakers loud and clear. "I got the heavy-duty bolts to attach the swing after I pick it up. I figured we'd choose a spot tomorrow and that way the boys and I can hang it when I bring it home on Wednesday."

"I love that idea."

"And I made supper."

Janet put her hand over her heart in an over-the-top reaction. "You are the best."

"You're not going to ask what it is?" he asked.

"I didn't have to chop, grill, or steam anything and we won't have any trouble getting to Jaxon's game on time. I'm good. See you in five minutes."

"I'll be here."

She disconnected the call and gave a peaceful sigh. "If we never figure out who NoPlaceLikeGnome is, I will still be perfectly content because..." She tapped the phone connection on her steering wheel. "I've got him."

"You sure do." Janet smiled as she got out of the car, but she leaned back in before she shut the door. "But a quick reminder. We are getting close to running out of days in April. You did make a promise."

Debbie knew what Janet meant. She'd promised to have the wedding organized with a set date and all the arrangements that go along with it by the end of the month, and that didn't give her too many days left. "Now that we've had a beautiful Easter, I'll jump back on it. Okay?"

"Yes. See you in the morning." Janet waved as she headed for the house, but her reminder stuck with Debbie.

It was time to get those details nailed down. She would make that a priority this week, but as she pulled into Greg's driveway, admiring the beautiful gardens that some wonderful anonymous person had restored—there was another mystery!—Greg came out the side door to greet her.

When she saw him, she knew straight off why she'd been slow with pesky details. Not because she was hesitating.

She wasn't.

But being with him and the boys, sharing time with them, made everything else seem inconsequential. And that was a wonderful feeling.

CHAPTER EIGHTEEN

The rain cleared up overnight. Tuesday morning dawned with much-welcomed sunshine. Debbie donned a light jacket and decided to walk to the café from her little home. She was going to miss this place when she married Greg and moved in with him and the boys.

The town was quiet this early in the day. There was something about walking the village streets, seeing the forged metal bike racks, the beautiful pots for flowers, the gorgeous black Dennison benches that invited people to pause. To stop and sit awhile. Maybe chat with someone, whether an old friend or a stranger who might become a friend in time.

The village and the villagers had worked hard to renovate and update parts of the historic town, and people were noticing. She knew that because the café and other businesses were doing well. The village that had been known as "Dreamsville" was coming back to life, and she loved being part of that renewal.

She stowed her things once she got inside, called out a hello to Janet, and grabbed an apron.

She let out a cry when she turned back around. Not real loud but loud enough to bring Janet running.

Bernice Byrne stood at the counter, staring at Debbie as though she had two heads. She was certain that Bernice hadn't been there a moment before. How had she suddenly appeared out of thin air?

"I know you're not open yet."

A part of Debbie longed to ask what the elderly woman was doing here if she knew they weren't open. She didn't do it, of course. Businesswoman Debbie stifled the temptation and kept her voice deliberately calm. "Good morning, Bernice. Sorry the pastries aren't in the case yet." She slipped the apron on and tied it securely around her waist. They still had forty minutes before they flipped over the Open sign, but one look at Bernice's face told her something was wrong. Grievously wrong.

"Bernice, are you all right? Has something happened?" she asked as Janet came through the swinging door.

"Fred has disappeared."

"Fred?" Debbie glanced at Janet, puzzled. Janet seemed just as confused, so Debbie brought her attention back to Bernice. "Do we know Fred?"

"The cat." Bernice half mumbled the words. Her tragic expression was nothing like her normally stoic countenance.

"The cat you just rescued?" asked Janet. "The orange tabby?"

"Yes."

Debbie hesitated. In the two years since she'd been home, she'd never seen Bernice like this. The no-nonsense animal rescuer was gone, bested by an orange cat with a mind of his own.

Janet came around the counter. She didn't reach out to hug Bernice. They both knew Bernice wasn't a hugger, nor did she suffer nonsense from people, but her current situation smacked of desperation. "How can we help?"

"That's just it." Bernice groaned softly, then offered a weary sigh. "I don't know. I've never had a cat run off like this. In all my time rescuing them, finding them the right place to live out their days, this has never happened to me, and I've been able to place cats in all kinds of homes, you know."

Debbie nodded. She'd heard all the stories. Bernice's track record with cats was impressive.

"Sometimes they went to city people. Other times it was a house with kids in the country or on a village street. Even a few barns for those cats that liked their independence. You'd have expected problems with a cat like that, but Fred was different. Smarter. More intuitive. I knew that from the get-go."

Debbie fixed a cup of tea, and then she reached over and set it in front of Bernice.

Bernice sank onto a stool. Defeat weighted the old woman's shoulders, and that wasn't an expression Debbie was used to. Not where Bernice was concerned.

"We'll look for him this afternoon." She offered the help sincerely. She knew they'd intended on dropping by Bernice's house later that day, but Bernice didn't know that and didn't have to. Their focus had just shifted from figuring out inanimate garden decor to something very animated indeed. An orange-striped cat with a bit of wanderlust in his DNA.

"I didn't know you named the cats you rehome." Janet took a seat next to Bernice. She sat casually as if she had all the time in the world. She didn't, but the warmth of her tone and expression said otherwise.

"Never have before." Bernice stared at the floor then sighed again. "Just this once. I let myself do it just this once, and now this has happened. I don't know what to do."

"He looked like a Fred."

Bernice tipped her gaze up to Debbie's. She frowned, just a little. "You think so?"

"Absolutely." Debbie leaned on the counter from her side and folded her hands. "Something about the strength of his gaze."

"Yes!" Bernice brightened up noticeably. "He'd lift his chin and look right at you but not in a mean way. Just strong and steady."

"Exactly how I'd phrase it," Debbie agreed heartily. "He had a presence about him."

"You know your cats," declared Bernice.

Debbie wasn't sure what to say. She wasn't exactly a cat fancier, but there was something about the orange tabby that exhibited a strong nature. "I don't," she admitted. She didn't want to fool Bernice. "But Fred gave off that aura when he was around here, and even a non-cat person like me could see that. He's a good one."

"Except now he's gone, and all my tricks and wisdom haven't brought him back or even given me a sighting. I thought if he felt loved and secure he'd stay put in the house, so I let him out of the big crate."

"Well, that was a good first step for him, Bernice." Janet encouraged her with a look of compassion. "That sounds like a perfectly normal graduated process."

"I usually recommend that to other people when I drop the kitties off," Bernice told her. "I want the cat to bond with them, in their home. I messed up by letting him out too early, and now I don't know how to fix it. Maybe I can't."

"So you changed your protocol this time." Debbie leaned in a little closer.

Bernice nodded.

"May I ask why?"

"Because I was going to keep this one. He's special. For the first time ever, I was going to have a cat of my own."

"We'll come help," Debbie said. "We can probably get there by three. That gives us lots of daylight."

"A cat can go a long way in twenty hours," Bernice said, but the offer of help seemed to firm up her voice a little. "You don't mind?"

"Happy to help," Debbie declared. "Bernice, you've helped people and cats for decades. We are happy to do the same for you."

"Are you hungry, Bernice?" Janet stood but waited there for the answer. "We'd be glad to get you some breakfast on the house. You've got to keep up your strength if you're going to look for Fred."

Debbie hoped the offer of food would tempt the woman.

She shook her head. "I couldn't eat. My stomach gets twisted up when I'm upset so I try to not let things bother me. That's why helping the cats is important. Not just for them," she admitted. "It's good for *me* because I'm helping them to a better life. A doctor told me a long time ago that helping others was the best remedy for my nerve attacks, and I took his words to heart. It's worked," she added. "Until today."

"We'll be there as soon as we can after closing," Debbie assured her. "Is there anything special we should bring along?"

"Just good eyes and ears and maybe some tuna. Not the fancy stuff either. That fancy white stuff doesn't have enough smell, you know? Kitties like the oily stuff."

"We'll grab some on the way."

Bernice stood up.

She hadn't touched her tea.

She turned and trudged out of the café, head down, but the promise of help seemed to ease her somewhat. Now if only they could find the missing cat, that would be marvelous. But if they couldn't, at least their efforts might bring comfort to a woman who had helped so many over the years.

CHAPTER NINETEEN

*J*anet called Bernice as they approached Debbie's car a little past two thirty. A slow day of sales had left time for cleanup prior to closing. The benefit of that was getting on their way to Bernice's house in time.

Bernice hurried out of her house a few minutes later. The first thing Debbie noticed was the change in her countenance. This morning she'd looked defeated. Now the woman seemed driven. She had a fisherman's style hat on her head, a zip-up flannel jacket, long pants, and sturdy shoes.

Janet climbed out from behind the wheel. She retrieved three cans of chunk light tuna—in oil—from her back seat and handed them to Bernice. "Temptation is a wonderful thing, Bernice!"

"And this is the best. Beats those commercial cat foods, nine times to Tuesday."

Debbie had no idea what that meant, but it didn't matter. Bernice was on a mission, and she and Janet were there to help.

"I've got geographical assignments for each of us," she told them as she handed them slips of paper. Another car pulled up as she distributed assignments.

"People think you should call, 'Here, kitty, kitty.'" Bernice folded her arms and tapped her toe as someone emerged from the car that had parked two doors down. "That might work on the dumb ones. It doesn't do a thing for the clever ones, and I'm pretty sure my Fred is gifted. Gifted enough to give me the slip, anyhow." She made a face and rolled her eyes. "That puts him higher on the charts than most. Alicia, thank you for coming."

Debbie turned and there was Alicia Whitman, coming their way. She saw Debbie and hesitated. Then she drew a breath. She kept moving forward but didn't look comfortable doing it. She acknowledged Bernice as she drew near. "Always ready to help a cousin, Bernie."

They were related. Debbie hadn't known that.

Bernice didn't take time to exchange pleasantries. She handed off a small sheet of paper to Alicia. "This one's yours. You can go in the same direction with Debbie. She's not schooled on cats." She peered up at Debbie momentarily. "But she's got a good sense about them. And you know this area, Alicia, about as well as I do. Being raised over here gives you an edge."

If Alicia had thoughts about the assignment, she kept them to herself in front of Bernice.

"We're doing this on a grid," Bernice continued. "Just like one of those search-and-rescue shows. That way we know we've covered the whole area. When you get to the creek, turn around and come back. Then we'll go to the next block." She drew her shoulders up, raised her chin, and hauled in a deep breath. "Janet, you're with me. Let's go!"

Janet sent Debbie a quick look of concern. They knew how Alicia felt about Debbie's relationship with Greg, but there was nothing to be done. Not if they were going to be the best help they could be to Bernice.

Bernice and Janet headed east.

Alicia and Debbie went west on the narrow side street. They moved in silence for several minutes, looking this way and that, but by the time they got to the nearest crossroad, Debbie resorted to clicking her tongue in an attempt to lure the elusive Fred.

Alicia did the same thing.

Despite their combined efforts, they got nothing. No cats appeared. None meowed. The street stayed empty except for the occasional car or jogger, but Debbie noticed something. A very important thing that made this neighborhood stand out. Almost every house had at least one, and often more than one, cute garden decoration in their borders or along their hedges.

When they got three blocks away from Bernice's house, where the bridge crossed Claymont Creek, they turned around.

The awkward silence continued.

Debbie motioned to her left, then decided someone had to make the first conversational move. "Let's go back down on this side of the street. Or we could split up and call for Fred on both sides?"

Alicia sighed then faced Debbie head-on. "I need to apologize to you."

The formerly awkward silence was about to turn into an awkward conversation that Debbie really didn't want to have. Not now. Maybe not ever. But it was only right to listen.

"I've been a jerk," Alicia told her.

A part of Debbie wanted to smooth it over, let it go, but Alicia wasn't wrong. She'd been snubbing Debbie for the better part of a year, and that was rude.

"And it's not for reasons you'd expect," she continued.

Debbie frowned, but Alicia kept going. "My sister Emmy is divorced. She's younger than me. Just two years younger, but it seems like a lot more, if you know what I mean. She's got two great kids, but Emmy is a magnet for bad guys. Not criminals but self-serving and immature. The kind who spend their savings on Friday night and have nothing left for Monday morning. You just can't do that when kids are involved. There was this part of me that kept thinking if she could fall for a good guy like Greg, that would make all the difference."

"Wouldn't Greg have to fall for her too?" asked Debbie. She knew she'd made her point when Alicia flushed.

"You've just cited the fatal flaw in my plan. I selfishly wanted to save my niece and nephew from heartache, but wasn't thinking about what would be good for Greg's boys. As much as I love my sister, I don't know that she would ever put them first. She can't seem to put her own kids first, and that breaks my heart." She took a deep breath and sighed it right back out.

"I loved Holly. We were such good friends. We did everything together, and it was awful to lose her. But about the same time you came to town I got to thinking that if Greg and Emmy fell in love, he'd be great for her, great for her kids and it could work out all around." She paused a moment before continuing. "I was wrong. I hope you can forgive me for being stupid. I haven't seen Greg or those boys this happy in a long time, and I mean that sincerely. Please forgive me."

Her confession surprised Debbie.

"I thought it was because you felt like I was replacing Holly."

"I know." Alicia rolled her eyes. "That was an understandable assumption. I know no one can replace her. But there's no reason that Greg and the boys shouldn't find the best happiness there is. Paulette too. She was so good to me and Holly. Taught us a whole lot. I didn't expect to run into you today, and when I did, I figured it was God giving me a chance to tell you why I was behaving so poorly. And a chance to tell you it won't happen again."

A gentle relief swept over Debbie.

She wouldn't have said that Alicia's treatment was a major bother, but it had been sticky enough to make her want to avoid the woman. "I'm glad you told me. Yes, I forgive you. I also understand because I hate seeing kids in tough situations too."

"Good." Alicia drew herself more upright. "I'm grateful you're being so gracious."

"I'm glad we finally talked about this, Alicia." Debbie's heart felt lighter. She didn't know if she and Alicia would ever be friends, but at least they could be friendly.

"Me too."

Debbie was pretty sure Alicia hadn't taken the gnomes. Sure enough that she didn't want to ask and possibly destroy their fresh, fragile truce.

But there was one question Debbie *did* need to ask. If her suspicions were right, she owed Alicia a thank-you along with the forgiveness.

"Alicia, are you part of the Weed Stealers group? The people who restored Holly's gardens at Greg's house?"

Alicia seemed about to deny it, but then she gave a sheepish smile. "Busted. I wasn't really sure how to approach you to apologize and wish you and Greg and the boys well. I realized how wrong I've been, and I wanted to make it up to you somehow. So I recruited Cecily Haygood, and we spent a morning doing the work while you were all away. I hope you don't mind. Looking back at it now, it's pretty intrusive digging up someone's yard without permission."

"Maybe it *was* a little intrusive," Debbie said, then laughed. "But when I saw it I felt nothing but relief and joy. The meaning was even deeper for the boys and Greg. What a beautiful gift to us all. Plus now I won't have to interrogate the neighbors about what they saw happening, which I would have gotten around to eventually."

Alicia visibly relaxed. "Cecily and I—mostly Cecily, because you know what a force of nature she is—swore them all to secrecy. She and I are talking about making the Weed Stealers a real community organization now. But we'll get permission from the homeowners next time."

"What a lovely idea!" Debbie responded. "And let me know if I can help."

"I will. Now shall we get on with this and find this elusive cat? I can't remember Bernie ever allowing herself the luxury of an animal or a pet. Something about this one called to her, and the fact that he disappeared is way more trauma than my elderly cousin needs. Bernie's got some odd ways and she's had to write herself notes to remember things for decades, but there are a few of us that love her to pieces. She stood strong when our family fell apart thirty-some years ago. If it weren't for her, I would have barely graduated high school, much less college with a degree in accounting. She helped shape my life and a bunch of others, so if finding this cat is a priority, I'm all in."

"Bernie is a Dennison treasure. Let's find Fred."

They went down all three blocks on the south side of the road with no sign of Fred or any other cat. They shifted to the next block, following Bernice's map. They hunted one full side and were half-way done with the opposite side when an orange blur streaked out from beneath a nearby porch.

It was a pockmarked wooden porch with trellised sides. The old paint was chipped and worn. Wind, rain, sun, and snow had done a number on the lower edge of the trellis where it met the ground. The elements—likely with some help from nest-seeking four-legged friends—had eaten away the lower part of the trellis. The gaping hole might have been encouraged by foraging woodland creatures looking for a winter hide-out or a summer nest. Sure enough, when Fred turned their way, he appeared quite self-satisfied as he purposefully trotted up the road.

"Oh my stars." Debbie stared at the cat before shifting her attention to Alicia. "That *is* him, isn't it?"

"According to the picture she sent me, it sure is. Look at that swirly coat pattern. I think he's been off hunting. What a clever boy!"

The big orange feline moved down the street, as if daring them to follow. When he got to the neighbor directly behind Bernice's bungalow, he made a smooth left turn, ducked under the back hedge, and disappeared.

"Should we cut through the yard or go around the sidewalk?" Alicia asked.

"I'm not losing sight of him at this point. There's no fence." Debbie pointed toward the hedge. "Just a stand of nice, friendly bushes. Come on!" She led the way up the drive and through the narrow pass-through and there—on Bernice's little patio—was Fred.

He sat there, nonchalant, thoroughly enjoying the afternoon snack of tuna. The self-reliant feline seemed comfortable there. As if hanging out on the deck was his thing.

"He likes his freedom."

Debbie couldn't deny Alicia's words. "I think you're right. Maybe he's the kind of cat that likes to come and go of his own free will." She texted Janet that they'd found Fred.

Janet's return message came through quickly. BE RIGHT THERE! Their walk back gave Fred just enough time to finish his afternoon snack. The cat then stretched out along the path of an afternoon sunbeam. The sun must have warmed the concrete to Fred's liking. Content and full, he took a deep breath, lazily raised a paw to his face—licked it once—and dozed off.

"Now that's the life." Alicia muttered the words, and Debbie couldn't disagree. A snack and a nap were a wonderful pairing no matter what age—or species—you were.

Bernice and Janet arrived within minutes. The orange cat's purr could be heard several feet away.

Bernice broke into a broad smile when she spotted him. Then she looked from him to the door and back. "This won't do," she told the ladies.

They exchanged glances, uncertain.

"Debbie, can you get Greg over here as quick as he's able?"

Debbie wasn't about to argue. "Of course."

"I'll have him get what he needs, and we'll fix things up right for this boy," Bernice continued. "A cat door." She offered a sage nod to the three women, then pointed to the back entrance. "Right here. Then Fred can hunt as needed and return to his home when his day is done. The thing about cats…" She leaned in as if sharing a state secret. "You've got to know what *they* need. Not what you need. If my Fred's a hunter, then let the vermin of northern Dennison beware." She made the explanation *sotto voce*. "Not one person around here will feel bad to have a good hunting cat on hand. Not with the mice and vole problems we're having lately. Welcome home, my boy." She said the words softly and didn't try to approach the cat. Not now that she seemed to understand his missions. "Debbie, Janet, thank you for all you've done to help. This is a wonderful day, isn't it?"

Debbie had to agree.

She'd found peace with an old friend of Greg's, and they'd figured out the cat's disappearing act. Altogether a successful day. "Marvelous, actually. And you know what I noticed up and down these streets?" Debbie indicated the neighborhood with a wave of her hand. "Almost everyone has some kind of cute ornament or ornaments in their yards. Lovely, don't you think?"

"Oh, that."

Debbie and Janet exchanged glances. Then, when Bernice motioned them to follow her, Debbie's pulse ramped up. Was she about to reveal what was going on in her garage?

They all followed Bernice around the house. When they got to the driveway side, she opened up the bay to her garage. Debbie sucked in a breath and peeked inside.

Greg had been right.

There were dozens of yard ornaments and sculptures, flags, and signs filling the garage bay. They were somewhat sorted. Fencing in one area, statues in another, flowers and whirligigs in a different part yet.

Debbie and Janet exchanged looks, because this was exactly what they'd been hoping to see. Despite that, it wasn't what they'd expected. None of these yard treasures matched what NoPlaceLikeGnome had been using.

Bernice walked in and picked up a section of miniature picket fencing. It wasn't pretty. Then she pointed directly across the street. The neighbor's yard had been decked out with half-a-dozen pieces of this decorative fencing. Half were painted bright white while the others were a sharp minty green. The neighbor had alternated them with space between them and the effect was whimsical and sweet.

"They all looked like this last fall," Bernice held up the worn piece of fencing as she explained what she was doing. "I fix them," she went on. "That's how I get through the winters. I have a back room that's just for painting and trimming, but spring is the best time for foraging curbs and dumpster areas. I take the old things I find and I fix them up and sell them. That's how I can afford to help people when they adopt the cats I find. Not everyone has money for spaying and neutering, so if I have a little put aside from the yard decorations, I use that to help out."

"Bernie, that's wonderful!" Alicia looped an arm around the old woman's back. "I had no idea you were doing that! It gives these things a second life. I think your neighborhood would absolutely win the award for the cutest one in town. People are really getting out and taking care of things. What a perfect double service to the cats and the community!"

Bernice blushed, but she brushed off Alicia's compliments brusquely. "Well, we don't need to get all on about it, you know. I can't stand seeing useful stuff going to landfills. So I save them and give them another chance."

"I agree with Alicia." Debbie wouldn't have expected those words to come out of her mouth a few hours before, but she'd learned another new thing today. It paid to look deeper to get to the root of people's actions. She and Alicia had gotten there today, and they both seemed to feel better for it. "I'm impressed by your efforts, Bernice. If you have time, I'd like to order some of that fencing myself." She pointed to the green and white display across the street. "If you've got enough to make me six pieces like you did for your neighbor, I'd love to place them in our gardens this summer."

"I sure do." Her request inspired Bernice's smile. "I've got plenty because people tire of this or that and set it out for pickup. Sometimes it's kids cleaning out parents' garages and thinking nothing of what they're throwing away. Of course their circumstances might be different or they've got no use for it anymore. What colors are you thinking?"

Debbie paused to think, then pictured Hans and Greta. The two little statues were clothed in denim blue, gold, and white with splashes of cranberry. "How about white and blue?" Bernice nodded.

"A medium blue." She added the shade because the spectrum of blues ran deep. "Like faded denim. I think that will go well with the little statues we have. When they get returned, of course."

Alicia frowned. "Hopefully nothing happens to them. Although like everybody else, I do like the stories I see posted. Whoever has them has been having a lot of fun. They're so creative, aren't they? They remind me of those stories my kids read when they were like eight and nine. The Fisher Kids Adventures. They couldn't wait for those books to come out to find out what the Fisher twins were up to next. I didn't think I'd like fantasy for the kids, but these were funny and well done and made them laugh. I get the same feeling when I see these posts shared on the town's profiles. Like we're in the middle of a fun chapter story and never sure what's going to happen next. I think the attacking leprechauns scenes were my favorite."

"Mine too," admitted Janet. "And seeing Hans plotting how to handle them was so funny, especially up on the railroad cars. Someone is clearly clever as well as skilled."

Debbie had texted Greg about Bernice's request. He texted back that he'd fit her job in first thing in the morning. When she shared that news, relief softened Bernice's features. "I'm going to bring Fred in for the night," she told them. "And let him get used to the pet door later tomorrow. It's clear he knows his way around and comes back where he now belongs, so I'm going to trust his instincts to know what's right for him. I'll trust mine to know how to keep him safe. A cat's got to know he's welcome even after a bit of wandering, and that's what I aim to do."

They said their goodbyes.

Once they were on their way, Janet said, "So. How did it go with you and Alicia? Because things seemed more comfortable when we got back to the yard."

"They are." Debbie offered a sigh of relief. "By the time we were done talking, I realized it pays to give others some leeway. Our talk reminded me that assumptions are often misguided. Good rule to remember."

She didn't reveal what Alicia had said, and she wouldn't, even to Janet, unless circumstances warranted it. But if there was ever a time when Alicia's little nieces needed some extra care, she wanted to help. She texted that message to Alicia that night, and when Alicia's return text came through, Debbie knew she'd done the right thing.

THANK YOU. IT MAY COME TO THAT, AND I WON'T PRETEND I DON'T APPRECIATE THE OFFER. SOMETIMES A LITTLE HELP IS ALL IT TAKES TO KEEP A KID ON THE RIGHT ROAD. MY SISTER MANAGES TO PUT PEOPLE OFF WITH HER ACTIONS, BUT THOSE CHILDREN ARE A BLESSING. I TRY TO MAKE SURE THEY KNOW THAT. IF A CHILD FEELS SPECIAL, IF THEY FEEL LIKE SOMEONE'S GOT THEIR BACK, THAT'S A GREAT INDICATOR OF FUTURE SUCCESS. GOD BLESS YOU!

Debbie had woken up that morning to one reality. A lot had changed in the course of one day, and all of it for the good. This new peace with Alicia, a woman who not only knew Jaxon and Julian but who'd known their family for decades, was an unexpected blessing. Added to that, the fact that a woman with a heart of gold brought them together simply showed the Holy Spirit's hand at work. She typed back three little words:

AND YOU TOO.

CHAPTER TWENTY

What have we here?" Debbie paused as she came through the Connors' kitchen the next afternoon and spotted Julian crouched beside two good-sized cardboard boxes. "Someone moving?"

Julian rolled his eyes. "Dad said I have to go through old stuff and decide what to keep and not keep because I'm possibly a pack rat. Whatever that is."

"A very busy rodent who loves to hang on to things. I have a smidge of pack rat in me too." She knelt on the floor next to him and checked out the boxes. "I keep sentimental things," she confessed. "And things I love, especially books." She made that admission as she tapped the stack of paperbacks in the second box. "I have what I call my 'keeper shelf' in my living room, except it's not a shelf anymore. It *started* as a shelf and has expanded into a full-on four-foot-tall bookcase."

"Have you read them all?" he asked.

Debbie nodded quickly. "Sure have. That's how they made it onto the keeper shelf. I loved them that much. And for your information, my friend, that bookcase includes some of those angst-filled favorites you were complaining about a few weeks back."

"Books that make you cry." He made a face when he said it.

"Yes, sir. I have half a dozen or so on my shelves. Rite of passage books. Including *The Yearling* and *Where the Red Fern Grows*. What are these books here?" She motioned to the stack she'd tapped.

Julian lifted the top book. His eyes lit up. "Fisher Kids Adventures. I loved these books back in fourth grade. They're about these kids that get into all kinds of trouble and mysteries that happen with weird creatures and characters from all over. Like all over the universe and time. History, myths, legends."

"How funny," Debbie said. Julian gave her a questioning look. "I've lost track of how many times I've heard about those books in the last few days. You mentioned them a while ago too. Just yesterday Mrs. Whitman said something about them. Twins, right?"

"Yeah, Sadie and Sam. They were always getting into something. B.B. Baldwin was my favorite author for about two years. He couldn't write books fast enough to keep me happy." The memory made him smile. "I would bug Dad to keep watching on his computer to see if a new book was released. And he came to talk at our school when I was nine," he added.

"Our little school got a big author like that to come and do an author day?" She raised her brows, surprised. "That's pretty cool, Julian."

"Well, he was coming for something else, I guess. I remember Miss Priestly saying something about him being almost a hometown boy but that he lived in a big city. One of the Pennsylvania cities, I don't remember which one. Anyway, Mr. Hancock heard about it and asked him if he would come, and he said yes."

Joe Hancock was the current elementary school principal. He'd been two years behind Debbie and Janet in school.

"It was really fun because he's a funny guy." Julian picked up the top book as he shared the memory. "Everything he says makes you laugh. Even when he's making you think, he makes you laugh. I like laughing over a book more than crying."

"I hear you." She picked up the next book in the pile. It didn't take long to see why Alicia saw a resemblance to their online story. The twins and all the supporting characters in the books were well drawn. They were thrust into a land of make-believe, fantasy, and intrigue, and while some of it was outlandish, it worked and didn't seem at all out of line with their faith, which was an important element of the Fishers' story. "How many books do you have of his?"

"Seventeen."

"Are you sure you want to get rid of them?" she asked. "I'm pretty sure your dad didn't mean for you to give away things that mean a lot to you."

"I thought about that, but I remembered what Pastor Nick said in church on Sunday. How sharing with others is better than keeping things for ourselves. I thought there might be some kid out there whose mom and dad can't afford to buy them seventeen new books. But if I donate them to the thrift shop, maybe someone can afford to buy their kid seventeen books that are only fifty cents or a buck. That seemed like a better thing to do."

Pastor Nick would be happy to hear that his words had been turned into actions and that the actions were those of a teenager. "I love how you think, Julian. Do you want to put them in my car? We can drop them off tomorrow. I can do it after work, or I can come get you and we can do it together. Mrs. Kendrick will appreciate them.

She calls people to tell them when someone donates things that she knows they're looking for."

"So she might know someone with a kid in elementary school that would love them?"

"Yes."

That thought deepened his smile. "That's cool."

"Yeah. It is. You're sure you're okay with parting with your collection?"

"I think so. Yeah. I'll put them in the back of your car, okay?"

"It's open. What time are you supposed to be at the field for the game?"

"Twenty minutes."

"Then we'll leave in five."

"I'll get my bag in the car too."

By the time he'd loaded his baseball equipment and the donation boxes, it was time to go. Debbie locked the doors to the Connor house and headed for the field. Jaxon had an away game that day. That meant they were doing the divide-and-conquer parenting routine. Greg was at Jaxon's game. She and Paulette would be at Julian's. With the games divided, there weren't as many spectators in the bleachers. She met Paulette on the uppermost level, ready to cheer the team on.

Five minutes into the first inning, her phone posted an alert from their new doorbell camera.

Someone—a man, nondescript, brown hair, head down and face turned away from the camera—was in their yard. Then their garden.

He walked quickly, as if he was *supposed* to be there, but he wasn't supposed to be there. He'd parked his gray car in the drive-way, fairly close to the house.

He went to the front garden. Debbie jumped up. "Paulette, he's there. In our yard! Look! Keep me posted on the game. I've got to go!" She flashed the screen in front of Paulette before she headed down the bleachers.

There was no way to get Greg from where he was, and borrowing statues wasn't exactly a police matter. Was it? No, but it was a curiosity matter!

She called Janet. Her business partner was a whole lot closer, and she'd understand Debbie's reluctance to get the law involved. Even if the law was her best friend's dear husband.

Janet answered on the first ring. "Hey, what's up?"

"Mystery guy is at Greg's house right now! Can I pick you up and we'll see if we can track him down?"

Janet's response was even better. "I'm actually right around the corner from you because I had to pick up a few things for Tiffany at the drugstore. Pull up to the curb, and I'll jump in. I'll ride shotgun with you anytime!"

Debbie was there within three minutes. Janet hopped in.

"Which way do we go?" Debbie headed for the light at the corner, but which way should she turn? Right? Or left? "How far would he have gotten in the five or six minutes it took us to get here from my phone alert?"

"Head toward Greg's house, and we'll watch for the guy's car."

"Yes!" She turned left. If he headed south, this was probably a wild goose chase because he'd be well ahead of them, but if he came through their small village, the chances of passing him were much higher. Not great. But—

"Debbie, gray Subaru coming our way!"

Debbie and Janet were heading south. The Subaru was going north. As they passed it, Debbie saw that it had one occupant. A man, light brown hair. A man who looked somewhat familiar, but she only got a quick glimpse because she was driving in the opposite direction.

"Is that him?" Janet asked.

"I can't tell, but it sure could be. There's something else, Janet." She made a swift U-turn at the next intersection and headed north. "Remember when I saw Bernice going through stuff on the curb and called you?"

"Of course."

"Well, I also ran into Rhonda Bontrager that day. Right there, at the pharmacy, picking up a prescription for Ephraim with her nephew. Then they got into a gray Subaru."

Janet looked at Debbie. "The nephew?"

Debbie couldn't be sure. Yet. But— "Do me a favor. Look up B.B. Baldwin on your phone."

"On it." Janet typed the name into the search bar and took a deep breath. "*Children's book author and illustrator B.B. Baldwin was born into a Mennonite family in southeastern Ohio. Married with three children, he now makes his home in Philadelphia.* Debbie, his book cover looks similar to the pictures in the NoPlaceLikeGnome posts."

"They sure do." Debbie didn't have to rush to get closer to the gray Subaru. She knew exactly where it was going. When she pulled into the Bontragers' personal driveway fifteen minutes later, that's where it was. She angled her car just enough so that B.B. Baldwin wouldn't be able to make a quick escape.

She and Janet went to the door, side by side. Janet rang the bell. When the inner door swung open, they were face-to-face with a nice-looking guy in his upper thirties, brown hair, an easy smile, laughing eyes, and holding a spatula.

"B.B. Baldwin?" Debbie said.

The man hesitated for only a moment, shrugged, and pushed the screen door open. "Come on in. I was making Uncle Ephraim blueberry pancakes. Don't want to burn them. Aunt Rhonda would give me a good talking-to, and if you know her, you know that's true."

Debbie and Janet exchanged looks, then went into the house.

Ephraim was seated at the broad maple table between the kitchen and the living room. He spotted Janet, and a smile of welcome brightened his face. "Janet, it is good to see you again. Rhonda brought those cookies home from your place a week or two back. What a treat they were. It reminded me that I must listen to the physical therapist and get more limber, because if I start gaining weight, there will not be a cookie or cake to be found in this house. Rhonda will make sure of that."

"Good to see you, Ephraim. This is my partner at the café, Debbie Albright."

"You bought my last heart swing." He peered up at her over his reading glasses and nodded appreciation. "I saw the sales slip. Thank you. Another reason to get up and get moving, so I can make more. Those hearts draw in business. What are you two doing up here?"

"I think they came to see me, Uncle."

"Did they now?" Ephraim's smile broadened. "What have you done this time, boy?"

"They've discovered my alter ego."

"Ach." Ephraim shook his head. "The jig is up, eh?"

"So it would seem. Fortunately, my need for props is over, so the story can be told, and sold."

"You knew?" Janet folded her arms and eyeballed Ephraim. "You knew what he was about all the while?"

B.B. pointed toward the table with the spatula. "Take a seat. Let me turn the griddle off. Unless you ladies would like a blueberry pancake?"

"Does it come with an explanation?" asked Janet, but Debbie was pretty sure they didn't need one.

"I think these two gentlemen were in cahoots to make the town laugh, and draw attention to these nice swings and chairs," she noted.

Ephraim smacked his fist on the table, laughing. "Benjamin did manage to get several of our pieces into the stories. Without making it obvious, of course. And he came by at just the right time, when I was down and out. I was so close to getting better, then everything slid backward when my leg got infected. Things went downhill for weeks. Having Benjamin here made all the difference. Oh, can this boy make me laugh! And other people too, it seems."

"Now you know I was the one who took things," B.B.—Benjamin Bontrager—said. "It's something that's become part of my trademark, but I've never done it around here. Always in the Philly area or out West and even in my California series. The twins' family liked to vacation, you see, and those twins got a look at a lot of the USA and a glimpse of Europe too. What exactly did I take of yours?" he asked.

"The stars of the show. Hans and Greta."

"Which I just returned, and that's how you caught me." He moved to the kitchen and tested the griddle. The bit of oil sizzled and spat when he sprinkled it with water, a trick Debbie had learned from watching her father make pancakes when she was a kid. Benjamin poured a generous ladle of batter onto it. "I saw the doorbell cam."

"Did you ever think of just asking?" Debbie wondered. "You know, hi, I'm a children's author, and I'd like to use your things as props in my stories?"

"This builds anticipation," he told her. "If people know it's a B.B. Baldwin story, then they want to help direct the story. I haven't written a Fisher Kids Adventure in three years. I was afraid of being branded as a one-hit series guy, so I branched out with other books. They did okay, but once I came here this whole story came together so perfectly that I've drafted it into a full-on book. With illustrations. My publisher wants me to do five more featuring Hans and Greta. If that's all right with you?" he asked Debbie as he flipped the pancake over. "I left a letter at your place explaining everything."

Which she hadn't seen because she was in such a hurry to catch the driver of the gray car.

"I didn't want to say yes to the contract without your okay. Those two little statues aren't like anyone else's yard ornaments," he continued, watching Ephraim's pancake carefully as he spoke. "They're unique. That's what made that story shine."

Debbie wasn't so sure. "You made the story shine," she told him. "You brought them and their adventures to life. But as far as using the statues, they're not really mine. They belong to my fiancé and his two boys. However, if you're willing to help me with a little surprise visit from my youngest soon-to-be stepson's favorite author this Saturday, I expect they'll run to jump on board."

"I love meeting the kids. They're the best part of the job." Benjamin slanted her a grin. "Are there Jan Hagel cookies involved? Uncle Ephraim wasn't the only one who fell in love with those."

"There can be," Janet assured him.

"I can't say no to good cookies. Or kids who love my books."

Debbie stood up. So did Janet. "I'm going to run it by their dad first," she told them. "But, Ben, I think your idea of using Greta and Hans for books might be the best bridge into the future for a boy who's been missing his mother for years. That would be an amazing way to bring this whole thing full circle."

CHAPTER TWENTY-ONE

Greg stopped into the café around eleven on Saturday morning. Business had been steady, but a midday lull had descended. Debbie spotted him as he came through the door and went to greet him. "You picked the perfect time for coffee. We're way too quiet here."

"Good for me." He winked. "So coffee, yes. And I have a question for you. A request."

"Hmm." She started to pour his coffee, but he stopped her with a gentle hand to her wrist. "Can I have that in a to-go cup, please? And can you take a quick walk with me?"

Debbie glanced around. Janet was compiling a grocery order for her father to pick up for them. She must have heard Greg's request, because she waved a casual hand their way. "We've got this."

Paulette agreed. "Nothing Janet and I can't handle."

Greg lifted one eyebrow in question. How could she say no? She put a lid on his coffee, hung up her apron in the kitchen, and met him at the door. "A walk it is."

"And a question." He smiled at her, and when they'd gotten outdoors he took her hand.

Here she was, on a beautiful late-April Saturday, strolling through town with the man she loved. What could possibly make this day better? "Where are we headed?"

"You'll see." He squeezed her hand lightly. "I think the boys are going to be excited when they find out that B.B. Baldwin wants to do a series wrapped around Hans and Greta."

"And I think they'll be thrilled when he asks their permission." She waved to a couple of the local firemen as they passed the firehouse. "He called last night to double check the time."

"And you told him four o'clock?"

She nodded.

They'd reached the next block. Greg turned right and she took in a long, deep breath as they made the turn. "This is a perfect day." She squeezed his hand, the bright warmth of the sun a balm after a long winter and a cold, wet spring. "The sun, the breeze, the temperature."

"And of course, the company. Couldn't ask for better. Hence the question."

"Ask away."

He paused opposite the churchyard. "Marry me."

She laughed softly. "I believe that question has already been asked and answered."

"Today."

She stopped laughing and looked around. "What?"

He indicated the sun-swept churchyard with a jut of his chin. "Apple blossoms, spring flowers, gorgeous green grass. Nick's available, and between the donut shop across the creek and what Janet's got in the bakery case, I'm pretty sure we can set up a pastry bar that rivals anything we could have taken weeks to plan."

He wasn't wrong.

The slow day meant that their bakery case was full.

"Pastor Nick and Brenda said they'd set up the coffee and tea service, my mom said she'd oversee the punch bowl, and honestly, Debbie…" He met and held her gaze with the same steadfast look she'd fallen for over a year before. "What else do we need?"

Nothing.

She realized that as she reached up, looped her arms around his neck, and brought him down for a kiss. "I think that's more than enough."

"You're good with an impromptu wedding. Spur-of-the-moment? Not huge and imposing?"

Now she laughed again. "The fact that huge and imposing was what's been bothering me all along is answer enough for that. I have the dress. We have the suits. Food and drink, a great pastor, and just enough help to make it all run smoothly. And the most beautiful setting I can imagine, provided by Mother Nature." She kissed him once more. "I'm sorry Buona Vita won't get the catering job, though. But maybe Kim, Janet, and I can set up a fun event in a few months and have them provide the food."

"That's one of the many things I love about you, Debbie. Always thinking of others."

"Well, right now I am thinking about you, me, and the boys. I say yes."

"Really?"

"Absolutely. I need to head back to the café…"

He shook his head. "The only place you need to go is home. Your mom is there. She went over and let herself in just in case you said yes."

She drew back, even more surprised. "You told her?"

His smile grew. "I'm not silly enough to think I could pull this off without help. Let's just say that Janet and my mom have the café all set, they'll take care of getting the punch bowl and desserts to the churchyard, a half-dozen Scouts promised to put out chairs then put them away later, and Tucker's going to play DJ with Kim's vintage record collection."

She paused their walk back to the café parking lot. "You've really checked all the boxes?"

"I didn't like that you were worried." He shrugged lightly. "Nothing's worth that. Since we both just wanted to be married, it made sense."

Oh, it did. It made absolute, wonderful sense. They hurried back to her car. She got in, and he leaned down to sweep a quick kiss on her cheek. "That's your last kiss as a single woman, Debbie Albright."

She grinned up at him and tapped his nose. "Then I shall eagerly await my first one as a married woman."

Debbie took a moment to stare at the reflection in her mirror ninety minutes later.

She was a bride.

Here. Now. In Dennison, Ohio, her very own "Dreamsville," she was a bride, wearing the most beautiful gown and her grandmother's sapphire necklace. She touched the stones, which felt cool and smooth beneath her fingertips.

She hadn't expected this when she came back home. She'd resigned herself to a life on her own years before. Then something happened.

She'd been offered a great promotion in Cincinnati, the chance of a lifetime for a small-town girl like her. That offer made her take a good, hard look at her life, her time, and her choices.

She'd known what it would mean to be a vice president in the corporate world. She'd sat in on the meetings, had seen what her predecessor had to deal with on a daily basis. She'd witnessed the dedication and extensive hours it had taken the VP to do the job right.

But something had nagged her.

A small nudge that couldn't and wouldn't be silenced. A nudge that questioned if that job was what she truly wanted.

She had suddenly realized that it wasn't.

She'd wanted more. Less, actually. Less work, fewer meetings, less controversy.

She'd wanted…home.

Her mother walked into the room, interrupting her thoughts. "Oh, darling. You look beautiful. So absolutely, wonderfully beautiful."

Debbie met her eyes via the mirror. "No tears. We promised each other, remember? No tears because we don't have time to redo makeup."

Her mother swept the back of her hand to her eyes quickly. "Agreed! But you do look breathtaking. Greg Connor is one lucky man. Dad's got the car ready, and I believe there's a handsome groom waiting a few blocks away. Shall we go?"

Debbie gave the reflection one last look.

She was here. In love. Marrying a great guy with two wonderful boys. As much as she loved running the café with Janet, running her own business, that was simply a beautiful stepping stone.

This—*here, today*—was the dream come true.

Twenty minutes later she was safely ensconced in the bride's room at the church.

Someone played a keyboard. The notes of heartwarming hymns—her favorites—rang out across the open space. Spring birds chorused, joining the music of the day. When Debbie peeked out the door, the churchyard had been transformed. Nature had done her part, but someone had filled old-fashioned metal buckets with blossom-heavy apple limbs. A collection of unmatched vases dotted the grounds, each showing off a collection of spring blooms interspersed with baby's breath for an airy touch. The perfume of flowers hung softly in the air.

Someone had woven apple blossoms into the lattice on both sides of the white gazebo. And there, at the edge of the gazebo steps, was Greg. The boys stood on his left. Jaxon, as tall as his father, and Julian, rapidly catching up to both of them. They turned with anticipation when the opening notes of Wagner's "Bridal Chorus" filled the air.

Debbie stepped onto the broad step as Janet preceded her down the aisle in a lovely floral three-quarter-length dress. Not a tradi-tional matron of honor look, and she'd probably just pulled it out of her closet, but Debbie's best friend shone with a radiant happiness that almost—*almost*—matched her own.

The guests stood. For just a moment she couldn't see Greg or the boys. Then, with her arm tucked through her dad's, they turned the corner leading to the gazebo and paused.

There he was.

There *they* were.

Her very own dream come true.

"Ready?" Her father touched her hand.

"I am."

They moved down the aisle. Whispered well-wishes followed her progress, but she scarcely heard them. Eyes on Greg, she stepped in front of the gazebo. When her father offered Greg her hand, her heart didn't stop.

It soared.

They ascended the wide steps together.

Jaxon and Julian grinned at her.

Greg tucked her hand through the crook of his arm. "You look absolutely beautiful, Debbie."

She smiled. "You're looking very nice yourself. All three of you," she added to the boys. "We ready for this?"

Jaxon nodded.

Julian gave her a thumbs-up, and Greg patted her hand and gave her a wink as he turned them toward the waiting pastor. "More than ready."

It wasn't a long ceremony.

Debbie had promised herself she wouldn't cry.

She almost did when she dropped Greg's ring, which she pulled out of a pocket in her beautiful gown, but Julian scooped it out of the apple blossom display before she had time to react. "Here you go."

"Thank you."

He offered her his shy half grin.

Greg shoulder-nudged the boy. "Nice reflexes." That earned a chuckle from the assembled guests and even from Pastor Nick.

Pastor Nick blessed the rings and handed one to Greg. With the pastor's guidance, Greg repeated the timeless words in a firm and solid voice. "With this ring, I thee wed. To have and to hold from this day forward. For better, or worse. For richer or poorer. In sickness and in health, to love and to cherish as long as we both shall live."

Simple words, but they meant everything to Debbie.

Looking up, she said the very same words to him. Almost. On the closing line, she ad-libbed a little. "To love and to cherish you—all of you—" she added with a gentle look including the two boys. "All the days of my life."

Pastor Nick's face shone with approval. He smiled at them before making his happy proclamation of marriage. "And now, by the power vested in me, I now pronounce you husband and wife... and family! You may kiss the bride!"

Greg didn't need to be told twice.

He drew her into his arms and kissed her, then pulled the boys in for a group hug.

They'd done it!

As they went back down the aisle to the cheers of friends and family, it wasn't just relief that swept her.

It was joy.

Absolute, unmitigated joy.

"Well, Mrs. Connor." Greg slipped his arm around her waist for their first dance as husband and wife an hour later. "May I have this dance?"

"This and every one to come," she told him, then looped her hands around his neck.

Kim had organized the playlist for the afternoon from her extensive vintage record collection, and Tucker expertly played the music. The strains of the Andrews Sisters singing "I'll Be With You in Apple Blossom Time" filled the sunlit garden.

When Debbie glanced over, she saw Ray and Eileen sharing a shaded table near the gazebo. The music kept Eileen's feet tapping and Ray smiling. Harry sat opposite Ray, Crosby at his own feet, and the three old friends didn't seem to be at a loss for words. Patricia stood nearby, next to Kim. Their parents, Janet, and Ian all wore broad grins, and tears sparkled in more than one set of eyes.

All around them, friends and family—who had gathered at a moment's notice—waved and gave thumbs-ups.

"This is perfect." She whispered the words into Greg's ear and felt him smile in return.

"Sure is. And we're about to make a couple of kids really happy once this dance is over."

She peeked over his shoulder.

B.B. Baldwin was there. He stood along the edge of the grass, watching them dance. Just a few feet away were Greg's boys. Her boys now too. They'd already hit the dessert table, because they were holding plates and napkins. They were about to find out that their mother's garden statues would live on in stories for children and adults for decades to come.

She looked into his eyes. "We've managed to change our lives and theirs, change the café into a thriving business, and now the town will be immortalized as 'Dreamsville' in the pages of some great kids' books. Who could ask for more than that?" She posed the question in a whisper, and her beloved whispered right back.

"No one, darling. Absolutely no one."

Dear Reader,

I hope you had as much fun reading this story about the funny online adventures of some cute but random garden gnomes and ornaments as I had in writing it!

We sell all kinds of fun things on our farm. Blodgett Family Farm is a growing enterprise, and while our season is short—just nine to ten weeks each fall—we enter into it with whimsical gardens, fairy house hunts, gnome scavenger hunts, and dragons! We love a fair amount of whimsy and make-believe on our farm, and it was a natural progression to share that love with all of you.

Here in the north we treasure the short months of summer. Living on the shores of Lake Ontario, I can tell you our winters stretch into May, and October often treads on the heels of summer. Having a huge body of very deep water really affects everything that happens weatherwise, so we've learned to celebrate the good times, good weather, and the seasons with all the fun we can muster. Including (but not limited to) yard ornaments, statues, and other creatures.

The fun of this mystery was keeping it lighthearted, showing the grace of a growing family and digging up suspects where none really existed. I loved showing Debbie and Greg's wedding, working with the kids as characters, and giving Bernice some peace of mind by letting her have her very own cat.

I hope you loved this sweet romance and this whole series. And—as always—thank you so much for choosing our books, our stories! You bless us every time you do that!

Wishing you all the best,
Ruthy

ABOUT the AUTHOR

Bestselling, multipublished inspirational author Ruth Logan Herne has published over seventy novels and novellas. She is living her dream of being a published author, and in her spare time she is co-owner of a rapidly growing pumpkin farm in Hilton, New York. She is the baker-in-residence, the official grower-of-the-mums, and a true people person, so filling her yard with hundreds of people every day throughout fall is just plain fun!

She loves God, her family, her country, dogs, coffee, and chocolate. The proud mother of six with a seventh daughter of her heart and fourteen grandkids, Ruthy lives in an atmosphere where all are welcome, no mess is too big it can't be cleaned up, and food is shared.

A GLIMPSE of the PAST

The Andrews Sisters

"I'll Be With You in Apple Blossom Time" was only one of many beautifully orchestrated hits by this group of sisters. Born in Minnesota, Patty, Maxene, and Laverne got their big break kind of accidentally after recording a Yiddish tune. When they first signed with their record label, Decca, they decided to sing *"Bei Mir Bist du Schon"* but with a jazzy arrangement. The song was released after Christmas 1937, and within days was the most popular song on the radio. Ultimately, it would become the first million-selling record by a female singing group.

The sisters' fame skyrocketed during World War II. They worked tirelessly, performing in person, making movies, and participating in USO concerts worldwide. The iconic "Boogie Woogie Bugle Boy" is probably their most famous song, joyful and danceable. But their crooning-style tunes like "I'll Be With You in Apple Blossom Time" recognized the loneliness of being separated from loved ones during wartime yet gave hope for a loving future.

The sisters went their separate ways in the 1950s, but the world has never forgotten them, their music, or the contributions their efforts made in keeping spirits up during the Second World War.

FROM the HOME-FRONT KITCHEN

Janet's Jan Hagel Cookies

Ingredients:

1 cup butter

1 cup sugar

1 egg, separated

2 cups flour

½ teaspoon cinnamon

1 tablespoon water

½ cup very finely chopped
    pecans

Directions:

Preheat oven to 350. Lightly grease a 15½ × 10½ inch pan. Mix butter, sugar, and egg yolk. Measure flour by dipping method or by sifting. Blend flour and cinnamon and stir into butter mixture. Pat into pan. Beat water and egg white until foamy, brush over dough, and sprinkle with nuts. Bake 20 to 25 minutes or until very lightly browned. Cut immediately into fingerlike strips measuring 3 × 1 inches.

Read on for a sneak peek of another exciting book in the Whistle Stop Café Mysteries *series!*

MY DREAMS ARE GETTING BETTER

BY JEANETTE HANSCOME

Janet Shaw hung a batter-splattered work apron on a hook in the Whistle Stop Café kitchen and studied her selection of 1940s-inspired smocks. As much as she could help it, flour and grease would not contaminate the darling aprons her mother had presented her with after church the previous afternoon.

"I found the patterns online." Mom had looked so proud when she handed Janet the tote bag. "I made five different ones for you, Debbie, and Paulette to share for the café's 'Throwback to 1945' countdown to Memorial Day."

An hour into the first Monday of May, cute aprons felt like the perfect addition to a month dedicated to honoring the eighty-year anniversary of Victory in Europe Day. Janet chose a blue-and-white gingham apron with a vintage image of a slice of cherry pie on one pocket and a frosted cupcake on the other. She grabbed two plates piled with breakfast goodness.

She nudged the double kitchen doors open with her hip and called for Debbie. "One stack of buckwheat pancakes with bacon and one calico scramble with wheat toast." She took a glance out the window to enjoy the morning sunlight. Only three days before, a freak May Day storm had soaked the area with torrential rain. Now, spring had settled in to stay.

Debbie swooped over from the cash register and whisked the plates from Janet's hands. "Thank you, ma'am. This will make some hungry customers very happy."

Janet tapped her foot to the rhythm of big band music playing over the sound system, compliments of the depot museum curator, Kim Smith's, extensive record collection. She admired the list of that day's throwback menu specials.

BREAKFAST – CALICO SCRAMBLE
(SCRAMBLED EGGS WITH BELL PEPPERS AND TOMATOES)
LUNCH – GRANDMA'S CHICKEN POT PIE
SOUP OF THE DAY – BEEF BARLEY
FROM THE HOMEFRONT BAKERY – VICTORY APPLE PIE

Scrumptious choices for the first full week of 1940s meals, baked goods, music, and red, white, and blue tablecloths.

After delivering the plates to a couple seated at a back corner table, Debbie returned to the area behind the counter. She stared at the Specials board as if not quite satisfied. She plucked a piece of chalk off the tray at the bottom of the board and added a pretty flourish to each corner. "There we go."

Janet took time to appreciate her friend's lovely chalk swirls. "Now the board looks as cheerful as the rest of the café."

Debbie brushed dust off her hands, taking extra care, Janet noticed, with the wedding ring Greg Connor had placed on her finger only a couple of weeks before during their whirlwind wedding. "I heard news that my husband and the Dennison Event Planning Committee recruited Tiffany to oversee games for the Memorial Day celebration." Her cheeks glowed a rosy shade of pink. "Is it weird that I love saying, 'my husband'?"

"No, I love hearing you say it." Janet was still getting used to thinking of her lifelong friend as a married woman. But she couldn't think of a better suited couple than Debbie Albright and Greg Connor. "Tiffany is thrilled to be overseeing games. It'll keep her plenty busy until her lifeguard job starts the first week of June."

"When is your girl coming home for the summer?"

"Sunday." Tiffany had given her the final rundown of her schedule when they video chatted on Friday night. "She takes her last final on Thursday, plans to do absolutely nothing on Friday, will pack on Saturday, and is heading home Sunday to celebrate Mother's Day and start her game-planning extravaganza."

Extravaganza seemed like the ideal word for what the Chamber of Commerce Events Committee was advertising as A Memorial Day Celebration of the Decade. In a few weeks, the Dennison Depot would be the end point for a parade and the home to a community picnic complete with classic carnival games set up in railcars, and a snack bar that Janet's former Third Street Bakery boss, Charla Whipple, volunteered to offer in the old Salvation Army Canteen.

Kim had just announced a half-price entry special for the Saturday before Memorial Day and created a Victory! exhibit dedicated to the end of World War II, open through the end of August.

Janet remembered a tray of peanut butter cookies that she still needed to add to the bakery case. "The Memorial Day event is going to be such a joyful lead-up to summer."

Debbie picked up a stack of freshly wiped down menus. "To add to the excitement, I have renters confirmed for the rest of this month."

"That's right." Janet opened the case in preparation for adding the cookies. "You have those students from Case Western Reserve staying at your place." It was exciting to see Debbie build a new life with Greg while still holding on to the craftsman-style home she'd bought from Ray Zink, by using it as a rental. For the next four weeks, Debbie would be hosting two graduate students from Case Western's premedical program, who were doing a project on the secrets of longevity among those ninety and over. They'd chosen Good Shepherd Retirement Center as their first focus group. "I hope your students include Ray and Eileen." Ray would turn 100 in June and still had a twinkle in his eye. Especially when Eileen Palmer walked into the room. Eileen was the picture of health and joy at 102. Then there was Harry Franklin, who'd celebrated his ninety-seventh birthday on April 22 and still lived on his own. "Harry would be a great candidate too, even though he doesn't live at Good Shepherd."

Debbie set her stack of menus beside the cash register. "Oh yes, go ahead and suggest him. He'd be awesome. I'm sure Jasmine and Amber will zero in on Ray and Eileen as soon as they walk into the retirement center. If anyone provides glowing examples of longevity at Good Shepherd, it's them."

Debbie went to the sink and filled a coffee carafe with water. "Jasmine and Amber are arriving tomorrow and plan to hit the ground running at Good Shepherd on Wednesday. The professor supervising their project has already paid the rent for May at my going rate."

"Lucky them. It sounds like their exam week ends early." Janet could still see Tiffany with no makeup on and her dark red hair in a ponytail, admitting to her typical pre-finals lack of sleep.

"Both mentioned having light course loads this semester while doing research." Debbie opened the top of the coffee maker and poured in the water.

Janet worked up the best impression of her mother from decades ago. "Have you met these students, so you know they aren't party animals?"

"Jasmine and Amber and I met via video call on Saturday night, and they are most definitely not party animals. More like some of the hardest workers I've ever spoken to. When they told me about their recent jobs and some of the courses they've taken, I felt like the biggest slacker of all time." Debbie reached under the counter for a bag of coffee. "They seem like great girls. Young women, I mean."

Janet started heading toward the kitchen for her cookies. "Anyone under thirty looks like a girl to me now that I'm nearing the tail end of my mid-forties. I still stock the cupboard with Tiffany's favorite cereal and junk food before she comes home for breaks."

Debbie plunged a scoop into the bag of coffee. "It's good to know I'm normal then. I took down a list of Jasmine's and Amber's favorite breakfast foods and snacks, even though I know they get a stipend for living expenses. They won't live on Ramen noodles on my watch."

"See, in a short time as a bonus mom of a fourteen-year-old and a sixteen-year-old, you already know the key to students' hearts. Snacks." Janet pushed one of the swinging doors.

The ding of the bell on the entrance triggered an instant turn of Janet's feet. At this time of morning, she always expected to see either Harry Franklin, his granddaughter, Patricia, or both. As predicted, Janet saw Harry at the door with his canine companion, Crosby. The cookies could wait. "Hello there, Harry."

"Morning, ladies." Harry swung his hips. "I like the music."

Debbie drummed on the counter. "Isn't it great? We should have a dance party."

Greg Connor was right behind Harry with his sons, Jaxon and Julian.

Harry led Crosby to the counter. He thrust his thumb over his shoulder. "Look who I found wandering around aimlessly in the parking lot."

Kim Smith came through the door next. "What timing. I showed up when all the cool people are here." She made a beeline to the counter.

Janet evaluated the contents of her bakery case. If this parade of regulars was an indication of what she could expect today, she might run out of the good stuff by midmorning. "I'm not used to seeing you here on a Monday, Kim." The Dennison Depot Museum was usually closed on Mondays, but Kim looked ready for a busy day in casual slacks and a blue cardigan.

Harry led Crosby to a table. "Did you decide taking Mondays off was for wimps?"

"Not exactly." Kim shot Harry a smile then moved her gaze to the bakery selection. "My Victory exhibit opens tomorrow. I still have one more display to finish."

Debbie took a tray of clean cutlery off a cart beside the kitchen door and moved it to the back counter. "I can't wait to sneak over to see the whole exhibit."

Greg came around the counter to where Debbie stood with a handful of spoons and forks and gave her a peck on the cheek. "Hi, sweetheart."

"Aw." Kim grinned at Debbie. "You guys."

Jaxon shielded his brother's eyes. "Dad. There are children present."

Debbie patted Greg's face.

Janet couldn't recall when Debbie looked more radiant. "They have special permission to be mushy for at least another month." She made a mental note to finally give Debbie the cookbook she'd made as a wedding gift. All she needed to do was wrap it.

Julian let his backpack fall into a chair at the table beside him and took a turn showering Crosby with attention.

Debbie squeezed Greg's hand. "What can I get for you?"

"I'll have a large coffee." He turned to the boys. "Jaxon, Julian, do you know what you want?"

Janet playfully tapped the bakery counter. "What can I tempt you boys with this morning? A common, ordinary cinnamon roll, or a vintage apple turnover fresh from the oven? I made some to use up crust from the victory apple pies."

Julian stood up from petting Crosby and went over to the case. "I'm torn. It all looks *so good*. I'm starving."

Greg's expression countered, *Are you kidding me?* "Didn't you just scarf down three eggs, a banana, two slices of toast, and a jumbo glass of milk?"

"I'm a growing boy." He settled on a turnover and orange juice. His brother ordered the same.

"So, young man." Harry gave Julian a friendly punch on the arm. "It's almost nine o'clock in the morning. Shouldn't you and your brother be at school by now?"

Crosby wandered over to Julian, dragging his leash with him.

"We have delayed starts today because of teacher meetings."

Jaxon joined his brother at the bakery case. "First period is at nine fifty for me and ten o'clock for Julian."

"We didn't have all those late starts and teacher workdays when I was a kid. Though I'm sure the teachers could've used a day off to work without us hooligans getting in their hair." Harry folded his arms across his chest. "I hear Julian's starting high school in the fall. Are you a genius yet?"

Julian wrinkled his nose and looked over at his dad. "I do okay."

"Yeah, I was a 'do okay' student too." Harry took a seat and slapped his knee for Crosby. He instantly ran over. "I could always count on an A in gym and history."

"I usually like PE." Julian sat with Harry. "But not this month."

Harry rubbed the space between Crosby's ears. "What's going on in PE that changed your mind?"

"Today we start a dancing unit. Ballroom and swing. *Ugh*."

Janet got bags for the boys' turnovers. "I remember the dancing unit. Tiffany loved it."

Kim did a little jig with her feet. "In school I would've rather gotten a grade for dancing than my running or tennis skills. Or lack of."

Greg put his hands on his son's shoulders. "He's just upset because the class has to perform for the parents."

"On Friday night of Memorial Day weekend." Julian made a face like he'd just swallowed something nasty. "It will be graded, and we have to wear formal attire. That's what Mr. Blake called it. Attire."

Jaxon smacked his brother on the back. "It's character building." He gruffed up his voice and expression to top off his grumpy old man impersonation. "I got through the dance unit and am a stronger person because of it."

Julian gave his brother the side-eye. "You tried to play sick the night of your performance."

Greg traced the seam of his cup with his fingers. "If I recall correctly, you pulled the old cliché faking a fever with a heating pad bit."

"I should've done better research. I gave myself a hundred and six temperature." He shook a finger at his brother. "But, in the end, I did the performance like a man."

Greg took two sugar packets from a basket on Harry's table. "Upon penalty of being grounded for the first week of summer break."

Debbie held three half-and-half cups out to her husband. "Well, I'm looking forward to the performance. It'll be my first school event as one of the parents."

"Here's a change of subject I think you'll all enjoy." Greg took a sip of his coffee. "How about if I let you be the first to hear a big announcement?"

Harry's eyes lit up. "Julian's class is going to lead the Memorial Day parade with a song-and-dance number?"

"Fortunately for Julian, the high school marching band is leading the parade."

Julian let out a loud sigh of relief.

"We need to cross our fingers that the band doesn't lose half its members to suspension for senior pranks."

Jaxon cut in, "Some seniors set off the fire alarm last week. They got in big trouble."

"What happened to moving the principal's car to the top of the science building or putting red dye in the swimming pool?" Debbie asked.

"Oh, hon." Greg patted her arm. "Those pranks are so two decades ago. Now for the announcement. The Chamber of Commerce met with our events committee over the weekend, and everyone agreed that something was missing from the Memorial Day parade. We have groups lined up to march and contribute the usual floats, but nothing exciting to set the parade apart from other years. So we are adding a float competition. The winner will get a trophy, and of course plenty of exposure in the *Gazette* and the local news. If the competition goes well, we might make it a regular thing and pass the trophy on to each new winner."

Julian smoothed down his hair. "That sounds cool."

"Can anyone enter a float?" Jaxon asked.

"Yep. Groups just need to register so we know how many to plan for." Greg peeled back the cover of a half-and-half cup. "I wrote an announcement for local businesses and clubs that will go out this morning. I'm planning to enter a float for Connor Construction. We're hoping to get all age groups involved." He poured in his half-and-half and opened another. "A list of requirements should go up on the Chamber of Commerce event website before noon. For now, I can tell you the floats need to either reflect the end of World War II, memorialize some who died, or honor those who contributed to the war effort."

Debbie leaned against the back counter. "The time frame seems tight. The parade is only four weeks away."

"That came up." Greg went over to the trash can beside the counter and tossed in his empty cups. "So we're making it part of the judging criteria—who can come up with something creative in a short time."

Janet glanced over at Debbie. "We should enter one for the café." A possibility started taking shape in her mind.

Kim stuffed some napkins into her turnover bag. "I wish I could enter a float for the museum, but I'm already swamped with the Victory exhibit. I have school groups booked all month long."

"Maybe I can draft you to announce the winner?"

"Count me in." Kim put her pastry bag into her tote. "I can't wait to see what everyone comes up with."

Janet bagged two more plump apple turnovers for the boys. She handed them across the counter to Jaxon and made a run to the kitchen for containers of juice.

Once everyone had what they'd ordered, Janet remembered a tray of peanut butter cookies and a Victory Apple Pie cooling in the kitchen. "I better get the rest of my goodies out before the breakfast rush really takes off." She hurried to the kitchen. While transferring the cookies from the cooling rack to a bakery tray, she pictured herself and Debbie doing delicate queen waves from the top of a float, their hair in victory curls.

When she returned with the cookies, Julian was wedging his juice into the water bottle slot of his backpack. "I can tell you one thing. My float won't include dancing of any kind." He nudged Harry. "But yours could."

Harry stared up at the ceiling then down at Crosby, who looked up at his owner as if he had a great idea of his own. "Nah, I have something else in mind."

Jaxon unscrewed the cap of his orange juice bottle. "You know what you're doing already?"

"Sure do." Harry opened his menu. "It'll feel good to do this again."

Janet set her tray of cookies on top of the bakery case. "You've entered a float competition before? We learn something new about you every day, Harry."

"It wasn't a competition, just a celebration. In 1946, Dennison marked the one-year anniversary of World War II ending with a parade and community picnic. Eileen asked for my help with a float for the depot. The Chamber of Commerce couldn't have afforded a trophy back then even if they wanted to make it a contest. It was all about celebrating and being together."

Julian took his turnover out of the bag. "What are you going to do for your float, Mr. Franklin?"

Harry picked up his menu and shook his head. "Can't tell you. You might steal my idea."

"I would never."

"I'm just messin' with you. But my float idea is still a secret." Harry shut his menu with a smack. "I can't get too excited about it anyway. The whole thing coming together as I'm picturing depends on me finding something that I haven't seen in quite a while."

Janet watched Harry's expression. What could he possibly have in mind?

A NOTE FROM the EDITORS

We hope you enjoyed another exciting volume in the Whistle Stop Café Mysteries series, published by Guideposts. For over seventy-five years, Guideposts, a nonprofit organization, has been driven by a vision of a world filled with hope. We aspire to be the voice of a trusted friend, a friend who makes you feel more hopeful and connected.

By making a purchase from Guideposts, you join our community in touching millions of lives, inspiring them to believe that all things are possible through faith, hope, and prayer. Your continued support allows us to provide uplifting resources to those in need. Whether through our communities, websites, apps, or publications, we inspire our audiences, bring them together, and comfort, uplift, entertain, and guide them. Visit us at guideposts.org to learn more.

We would love to hear from you. Write us at Guideposts, P.O. Box 5815, Harlan, Iowa 51593 or call us at (800) 932-2145. Did you love *Apple Blossom Time*? Leave a review for this product on guideposts.org/shop. Your feedback helps others in our community find relevant products.

Find inspiration, find faith, find Guideposts.

Shop our best sellers and favorites at
guideposts.org/shop

Or scan the QR code to go directly to our Shop

**While you are waiting for the next fascinating story
in the Whistle Stop Café Mysteries, check out
some other Guideposts mystery series!**

SECRETS FROM
GRANDMA'S ATTIC

Life is recorded not only in decades or years, but in events and memories that form the fabric of our being. Follow Tracy Doyle, Amy Allen, and Robin Davisson, the granddaughters of the recently deceased centenarian, Pearl Allen, as they explore the treasures found in the attic of Grandma Pearl's Victorian home, nestled near the banks of the Mississippi in Canton, Missouri. Not only do Pearl's descendants uncover a long-buried mystery at every attic exploration, they also discover their grandmother's legacy of deep, abiding faith, which has shaped and guided their family through the years. These uncovered Secrets from Grandma's Attic reveal stories of faith, redemption, and second chances that capture your heart long after you turn the last page.

History Lost and Found
The Art of Deception
Testament to a Patriot
Buttoned Up

Pearl of Great Price
Hidden Riches
Movers and Shakers
The Eye of the Cat
Refined by Fire
The Prince and the Popper
Something Shady
Duel Threat
A Royal Tea
The Heart of a Hero
Fractured Beauty
A Shadowy Past
In Its Time
Nothing Gold Can Stay
The Cameo Clue
Veiled Intentions
Turn Back the Dial
A Marathon of Kindness
A Thief in the Night
Coming Home

SAVANNAH SECRETS

Welcome to Savannah, Georgia, a picture-perfect Southern city known for its manicured parks, moss-covered oaks, and antebellum architecture. Walk down one of the cobblestone streets, and you'll come upon Magnolia Investigations. It is here where two friends have joined forces to unravel some of Savannah's deepest secrets. Tag along as clues are exposed, red herrings discarded, and thrilling surprises revealed. Find inspiration in the special bond between Meredith Bellefontaine and Julia Foley. Cheer the friends on as they listen to their hearts and rely on their faith to solve each new case that comes their way.

The Hidden Gate
A Fallen Petal
Double Trouble
Whispering Bells
Where Time Stood Still
The Weight of Years
Willful Transgressions
Season's Meetings
Southern Fried Secrets
The Greatest of These
Patterns of Deception

The Waving Girl
Beneath a Dragon Moon
Garden Variety Crimes
Meant for Good
A Bone to Pick
Honeybees & Legacies
True Grits
Sapphire Secret
Jingle Bell Heist
Buried Secrets
A Puzzle of Pearls
Facing the Facts
Resurrecting Trouble
Forever and a Day

MYSTERIES *of* MARTHA'S VINEYARD

Priscilla Latham Grant has inherited a lighthouse! So with not much more than a strong will and a sore heart, the recent widow says goodbye to her lifelong Kansas home and heads to the quaint and historic island of Martha's Vineyard, Massachusetts. There, she comes face-to-face with adventures, which include her trusty canine friend, Jake, three delightful cousins she didn't know she had, and Gerald O'Bannon, a handsome Coast Guard captain—plus head-scratching mysteries that crop up with surprising regularity.

A Light in the Darkness
Like a Fish Out of Water
Adrift
Maiden of the Mist
Making Waves
Don't Rock the Boat
A Port in the Storm
Thicker Than Water
Swept Away
Bridge Over Troubled Waters
Smoke on the Water
Shifting Sands
Shark Bait
Seascape in Shadows

Storm Tide
Water Flows Uphill
Catch of the Day
Beyond the Sea
Wider Than an Ocean
Sheeps Passing in the Night
Sail Away Home
Waves of Doubt
Lifeline
Flotsam & Jetsam
Just Over the Horizon

Find more inspiring stories in these best-loved Guideposts fiction series!

Mysteries of Lancaster County

Follow the Classen sisters as they unravel clues and uncover hidden secrets in Mysteries of Lancaster County. As you get to know these women and their friends, you'll see how God brings each of them together for a fresh start in life.

Secrets of Wayfarers Inn

Retired schoolteachers find themselves owners of an old warehouse-turned-inn that is filled with hidden passages, buried secrets, and stunning surprises that will set them on a course to puzzling mysteries from the Underground Railroad.

Tearoom Mysteries Series

Mix one stately Victorian home, a charming lakeside town in Maine, and two adventurous cousins with a passion for tea and hospitality. Add a large scoop of intriguing mystery, and sprinkle generously with faith, family, and friends, and you have the recipe for *Tearoom Mysteries*.

Ordinary Women of the Bible

Richly imagined stories—based on facts from the Bible—have all the plot twists and suspense of a great mystery, while bringing you fascinating insights on what it was like to be a woman living in the ancient world.

To learn more about these books, visit Guideposts.org/Shop